D0459577

Mendocino County Bookmobile
105 N. Main St.
Ukiah, CA 95482

Tin Can Homestead

TIN CAN HOMESTEAD

The Art of Airstream Living

NATASHA LAWYER
and BRETT BASHAW

RUNNING PRESS
PHILADELPHIA

Copyright © 2018 by Natasha Lawyer and Brett Bashaw

Hachette Book Group supports the right to free expression and the value of copyright. The purpose of copyright is to encourage writers and artists to produce the creative works that enrich our culture.

The scanning, uploading, and distribution of this book without permission is a theft of the author's intellectual property. If you would like permission to use material from the book (other than for review purposes), please contact permissions@hbgusa.com. Thank you for your support of the author's rights.

Running Press
Hachette Book Group
1290 Avenue of the Americas, New York, NY 10104
www.runningpress.com
@Running_Press

Printed in China

First Edition: May 2018

Published by Running Press, an imprint of Perseus Books, LLC, a subsidiary of Hachette Book Group, Inc. The Running Press name and logo is a trademark of the Hachette Book Group.

The Hachette Speakers Bureau provides a wide range of authors for speaking events. To find out more, go to www.hachettespeakersbureau.com or call (866) 376-6591.

The publisher is not responsible for websites (or their content) that are not owned by the publisher.

Illustrations and photographs copyright © 2018 by Natasha Lawyer, except those specified on pages 11, 20–21, 22, 25, 26, 34, 50–51, 60, 70–71, 75, 78–79, 98, 106–107, 116, 120–121, 140, 143, 148, 154, 156–157, 164–165, 167, 171, 172, 174, 178–179, 185, 210.

Photographs on pages 11, 20–21, 22, 25, 26, 34, 50–51, 60, 70–71, 75, 78–79, 98, 106–107, 116, 120–121, 140, 143, 148, 154, 156–157, 164–165, 167, 171, 172, 174, 178–179, 185, 210 copyright © 2018 by Ellie Lillstrom

Print book cover and interior design by Ashley Todd.

Library of Congress Control Number: 2017961719

ISBNs: 978-0-7624-9144-5 (hardcover), 978-0-7624-9145-2 (ebook)

RRD-S

10 9 8 7 6 5 4 3 2 1

Contents

THE BEGINNING

Our journey to tiny living began with a text. My husband Brett was driving to work, or rather, stopping for coffee and dreading arriving at work. While waiting for his order, he sent me a message, "what if we took a year off to travel?"

He told me later that this was prompted by a documentary he had recently seen, in which a rich and successful surgeon, who was suffering from depression and feelings of deep unhappiness, sold everything he owned in favor of buying a condo on a beach. After the surgeon quit his job and moved, he chose to spend his days in-line skating up and down the pier and was happier than he had ever been. In changing his life in such a drastic manner, the surgeon had shirked conventional ideas about what should make someone happy and successful. At that time, Brett was feeling stir-crazy and stuck in the day to day mundane—seeing that documentary only exacerbated his feelings. So, when he sent his text about quitting our jobs and traveling, he expected my answer to be something along the lines of, "yeah that would be nice, with what money?" Instead, I texted back, "what if we bought a van and lived in it?"

We both share a love of travel, so when I received Brett's text, I was game for that part of things. But, when I got to thinking about how we could make it happen from a practical standpoint, I realized that

"WHAT IF WE TOOK A YEAR OFF TO TRAVEL?"

paying for a place to stay is always the most expensive part of travel. But, if we brought a place to stay along with us, we could make it work.

Three months later we were the proud owners of an orange vintage 1978 Volkswagen van that we dubbed "Wes Vanderson." (Brett said it looked like a prop from a Wes Anderson movie when he found the advertisement for it; I came up with the name.) Ever the romantic, if I was going to spend six months living in a van, I was going to do it in classic Americana style.

We spent the next six months saving for time off and converting the van from a transporter to a camper van. Once it was finished, we took six months off, heading north from Seattle up through the west coast of Canada and across the entire country to Newfoundland—the easternmost tip of North America—then back down in a meandering crisscross all over the United States. We drove and hiked and read and explored and met people from all over. Many of those friends were acquired online, through our newly discovered community of "van lifers" on Instagram. We connected with people living in vans and recreational vehicles of all types, and as our trip began winding down, we started thinking about what our return home would look like. We had left Seattle at the beginning of the summer, handing back the keys to our apartment and putting everything we owned into a wooden storage pod. We couldn't afford to travel forever and we couldn't afford to buy the cabin we had dreamed of settling into one day, so where did that leave us? We were heading back to a wood crate filled with belongings we didn't miss in a city we couldn't afford. The idea of returning only to move into an overpriced apartment and work jobs that didn't pay a lot just to be able to afford to live in it seemed so awful. It felt like we'd be living just to pay bills. It seemed we would somehow be denying the transformative months we had spent living differently if we just settled right back into our old lives like the trip never happened. So we started brainstorming.

During our wanderings we had connected with a bunch of different nomad families through Instagram. Among those nomads were a couple of ladies under the Instagram handle *The Modern Caravan*. Kate and Ellen were traveling with their daughter in an Airstream, and I remember being so enamored with the way they had transformed their space. This was right around the time when I was sharing a bed that was only slightly bigger than a twin size with a six-foot-two-inch tall, broad-shouldered man and a dog. Both of them sleep like starfish, with their limbs splayed this way and that, which, among other things, was making van life seem less and less glamorous. In the morning I would untangle myself from a pile of limbs and then see a photo of a room

"WHAT IF WE BOUGHT A VAN AND LIVED IN IT?"

Photo kindly provided by Kate Oliver of *The Modern Caravan*.

with a gorgeous bed, piled with a fluffy ivory duvet beside a warm birch plywood sideboard and complete with a Chemex coffeemaker, nested in the middle of the woods somewhere. The contrast was stark. I remember being particularly obsessed with the above photo.

Up until that point every trailer and recreational vehicle I had ever seen was filled with dark wood laminate. Every inch, from floor to ceiling, was crammed with as many utilitarian cubbies as possible (not to mention the awful upholstery). And don't even get me started on showering above a plastic toilet. It's always been incredibly important to me that the spaces in which I exist are aesthetically appealing. Living in an RV seemed to contradict that inclination in

every way possible. But, after seeing the way those amazing ladies had transformed their space, it seemed plausible to take on RV life in style. Their space felt so light, airy, and modern—and they were pulling it behind them to places like Alaska and Joshua Tree. We loved how untraditional it was. I mean, they had a wood dining

room table with hairpin legs! (We had a similar one in Washington, sitting in a crate with everything else we owned.) And so we began to discuss how we could live in an Airstream back in Seattle. We imagined our-selves on a site in the middle of the woods in the Pacific Northwest, building fires outside and falling asleep in a regular-size bed.

Brett and I already knew that we did well living together in a small space; the Volkswagen was tiny, so the comparative size of an Airstream seemed huge. As we traveled from place to place, I began my research. I read Airstream forums about renovations and common problems; I discovered Airstream classifieds and perused them daily. We figured since we were heading back to Seattle in a couple of months, we could buy an Airstream wherever we found one and bring it back with us.

We spent a lot of time in coffee shops—and still do—as we're both coffee addicts, and Brett was enrolled in full-time university online. He would study, and I would endlessly scour the classifieds, drawing and redrawing Airstream layout plans. The first one I sketched out was in a coffee shop in Chattanooga, Tennessee, pictured above.

Besides deciding what the interior was going to look like and where we were going to buy an Airstream, we also had to figure

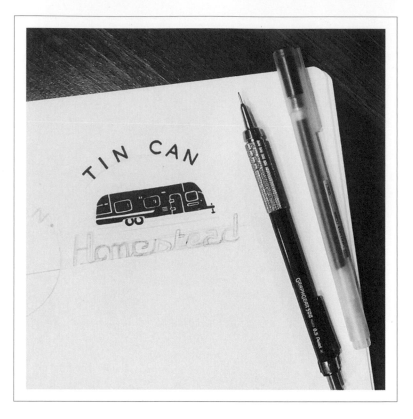

out the more important question of *where* we were going to put a trailer when we did find one. Obviously, buying a chunk of land was ideal, but we were going back to Seattle, and with the tech boom and the skyrocketing cost of land it seemed pretty unlikely that we could afford anything. Besides, while researching tiny living I discovered that you can't necessarily plop an Airstream or tiny home wherever you want and expect no one to bother you, even if it is your own land. I read about laws that prohibited living in tiny dwellings unless there was already a bigger house on a lot (and then what's the savings?) and learned that living in driveways full-time wasn't exactly legal either. I eventually arrived at the conclusion that an RV park was probably our best bet. I began to research parks within commuting distance of

Seattle. You don't have to drive too far outside of Seattle to be in the middle of the woods, and we needed a place we could live stationary and long term—a homestead.

In the meantime, I was researching what to look for when buying a vintage Airstream. I learned about the trailer frames (chassis) and common rust problems, about the fact that all Airstreams leak and what leaking is easily fixed and what isn't. I read about how many abandoned Airstreams become homes to mice, insects, and other vermin, which can mean that you will need to rip out all of the trailer's walls and insulation to remedy the problem. I compiled a little list of things to check out when we were viewing prospective new homes—I had read horror stories about people stepping right through rotted floors, or trailers coming away from rusted frames halfway down the highway

behind their towing vehicle. I also contacted our pals Kate and Ellen from *The Modern Caravan* and used them as a sounding board for shopping. They proved to be an invaluable resource throughout our process. Here's the checklist we came up with:

Things to Look for
When Buying a Vintage Trailer

1. **WATER DAMAGE.** All Airstreams leak. They're made of metal that's riveted together, and that leaves a lot of room for water to get in through the roof and window frames and each tiny rivet piercing the exterior. Check under and around each window and jump around on the floor to feel for soggy spots (we put a foot through one trailer we looked at). Open cabinets and look under things, as leaks can hide behind cabinetry and under beds and furniture. Replacing the subfloor is laborious, and it will start to sag with water damage, so look out for that.

2. **WINDOWS.** This is a big one for a few reasons. The first and most important reason is that replacing Airstream windows is crazy expensive. I saw a ton of ads in which someone casually mentioned that a few windows needed to be replaced, and I immediately moved on. The second issue concerning windows is that many models of Airstreams had a tinted coating inserted between layers of glass for sun protection. After about thirty years those coatings start to break down and flake, leaving you with horrible-looking windows that need to be replaced. Some restorers will try to break the inner layer of glass to scrape out the flaky coating, which sounds like a bit of a nightmare, so it's something to consider when evaluating a potential Airstream.

3. **SMELL.** As I mentioned earlier, abandoned trailers can become a home for pests and rodents, and a good way to determine if that is the case is to use your nose. In our Airstream, we had a pretty large area of insulation exposed where the shower had been ripped out, and we could see the state of things pretty well, but smells, particularly in insulation or near water sources, are something to watch out for. Some people may want to keep cushions or mattresses intact, so check those for smells too, especially mold. We were set on completely gutting our trailer or trying to buy one that was already gutted, so we weren't as concerned with that aspect of things.

4. **UNDERSIDE**. Check underneath the trailer to see the condition of the chassis or frame. Check the leveling jacks to find out if they're rusted out. Check the axles and springs for excessive rust. These are all things you will need to fix if they aren't in working condition, and those costs add up.

5. **TECHNICAL ISSUES**. Check that the Airstream is tow-ready. And when was the last time the brakes were checked? Are the tires in good condition? When were the bearings last repacked? Are the brake lights working? What about the turn signals? Check that the leveling jacks work and that the towing equipment is intact, including the exterior plug.

6. **TITLE**. It can be tricky and expensive to get a new title, so ask about it before buying an Airstream without one. Evaluate the costs of a new title and ask the seller to take that into consideration when pricing the vehicle. Also consider what excessive time at the DMV does to a person.

7. Depending on whether you're planning on gutting your trailer or not, check the following:
   - *Propane lines.* This can be dangerous if not properly done, so having a professional check it out for you before using is a good safety measure. Propane freaks me out a bit and we were planning on living on grid so we went with electric, but if you're planning on off-grid living, this is an important step.
   - *That all plugs and switches work in the interior.* (We completely rewired so we skipped this as well.)
   - *The condition of the AC.* Factor in the cost of a new one if needed. Those things ain't cheap.

Once I had this list to run over in my mind, I felt a little better wading through the piles of classifieds. The first Airstream we looked at was in rough shape, and the floor was so water damaged that Brett's foot went right through it.

One of the things that was important for us to determine early on was how much we wanted to renovate our Airstream. There are some people who buy trailers, leave the existing layout and furniture, and give them a cosmetic makeover: a new paint job, fabric change, appliance swap, etc. This requires a different set of guidelines when viewing the trailers. Some people tear everything out, including the walls, and take it right down to the studs and frames, removing the subfloor and even grinding down the frame. I knew I wanted to gut our Airstream entirely. I wanted to do all our own flooring, cabinetry, and appliances, and I wanted to customize the layout. But I also decided early on that I wanted to avoid taking the walls out if I

could manage it, and I wanted a subfloor that was mostly in good shape (instead of having to replace huge chunks of soggy subfloor). With those parameters in mind, I looked for an Airstream that was already gutted to save on demolition time and the expense and trouble of getting rid of all the interior materials that weren't needed.

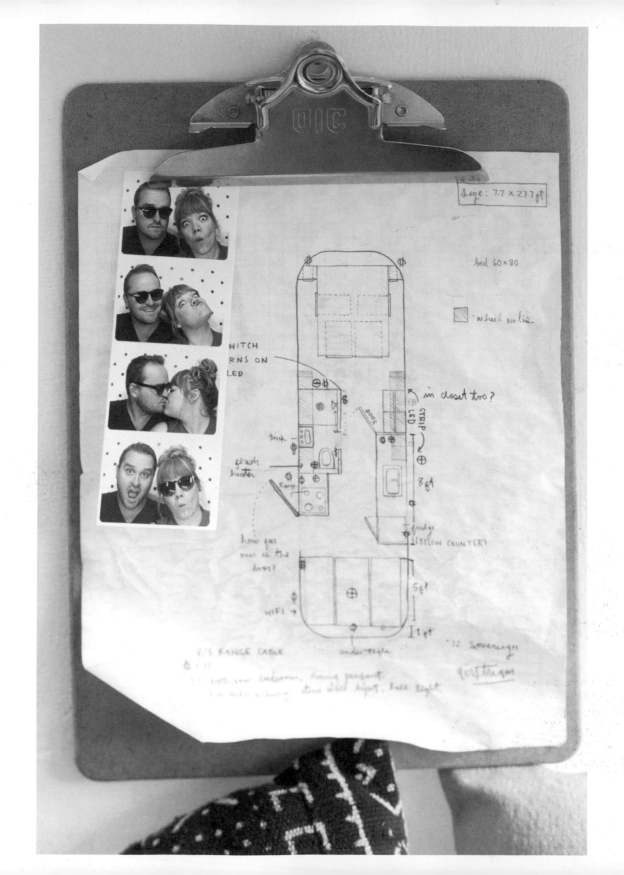

PLANNING

One of the first things I discovered about RV parks is that they're really hard to get into. Many of them don't allow long-term occupants, and if they do, there are restrictions on how old your trailer is allowed to be. Many have waiting lists and some do credit checks. I've seen a lot of school bus conversions lately that are beautiful, but most RV parks do not allow school buses, and they definitely don't allow tiny houses. These are all things to keep in mind when pursuing tiny living, and another reason why a travel trailer is a good choice. We got our spot in our RV park by the skin of our teeth due to a combination of my perseverance in cold-calling every RV park within a fifty-mile radius of

Seattle and Brett sweet-talking the manager the day of when she initially complained about the state of the Airstream on moving day. The other thing to keep in mind is that most RV parks don't want you renovating your trailer *at* the RV park. We parked our trailer in a friend's driveway for a month or so and worked on it a bit before towing it into the RV park. When we moved it in, it was an empty, scrubbed, painted, and primed shell with roller blinds (so the management of the park couldn't see that it was entirely empty). We didn't exactly have permission to be doing any renovations, but we kept our renovating to reasonable hours, were very friendly with our neighbors, and always made sure to clean up outside right when we finished our work for the day. Most people in the park were more curious than annoyed, and we invited quite a few neighbors inside to see what we were up to. But I'm getting ahead of myself . . .

After making sure we had a plan for a legal place to put our Airstream, we were able to firm up *how* we wanted to live in it. We planned to live stationary in our Airstream; we were going to live in an RV park so we didn't need to worry about getting power

off batteries or making sure our tanks were plumbed in for off-grid use. After six months of tooling around the country in our Volkswagen, we wanted to stay put for work—and sanity. Our future travel plans wouldn't include bringing our home. We basically wanted our Airstream to serve as a tiny house, and so we planned, wired, and plumbed it that way. And since I had decided that I didn't want to rip out all the walls, I worked on designing the interior in such a way that we could run all the electrical and plumbing through the walls and cabinetry we were installing. *How* you live in a space determines so much about

its design. If you love cooking, you prioritize kitchen space; if
you love guests staying with you, you make your layout guest-
friendly. If you have kids, they need places to sleep and play. How
much storage do you need? Are you renovating it to live in or just
for travel? Will you be using it as a mobile office; what kind of
a workspace do you need? These were all things we considered
when planning our space.

When we began the drawing and redrawing of our plans, I consulted common Airstream layouts and used those as a guide. We were still traveling in the Volkswagen at the time so I didn't exactly have the ability to draw things to scale or do any measurements, but drafting these rough multiple sketches helped me get an idea of what I wanted. Brett and I aren't big on cooking, so although I knew I wanted long countertops in the kitchen, we opted for additional storage instead of an oven because in previous apartments we'd had, we only used the oven once or twice a month. We also knew that we wanted to create a place where we could have guests crash with us for a night or two. In many of the Airstream layouts we were looking at, the bathroom was in the back of the Airstream. This meant that if we had guests staying overnight, they would be walking through our bedroom to get to the bathroom—not good. So, we decided to put our bathroom along the side where it could be accessed from the front and back of the Airstream. I spent a lot of time looking up photos of Airstream interiors and took notes on what I liked and didn't like in existing Airstream spaces:

LIKE	DISLIKE
— airy feeling	— clutter
— light colors	— dark wood
— good flow	— laminate
— lounge space separate from sleeping space	— rear bathroom
— light wood	— overhead bins
— long countertops	— propane (freaks me out)
— white	— too many colors in a small area
— storage	— master beds in front
	— climbing over someone to get in and out of bed (no sideways beds)

The natural flow of most living spaces is a *general to specific* layout. And by that, I mean public areas come first and gradually move to more private rooms. When you walk through the door of most houses, it doesn't open into the master bedroom; that would feel a little strange and personal. So, in the

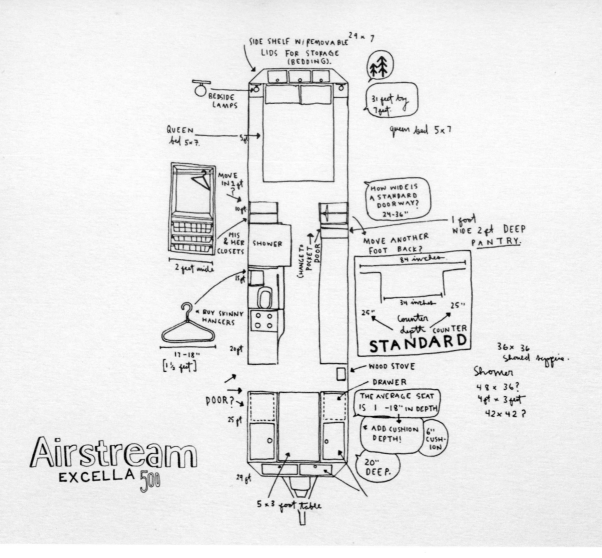

First draft of the Airstream floor plan. I could have used some graph paper so I could draw it to scale—the result was a floor plan that relied on quite a bit more length than we would have. The final plan didn't stray too far from this first draft though.

same way, I wanted to create a public to private flow in our Airstream layout. I had looked at Airstreams where the master bed was the first thing you saw when you walked in, but I knew I wanted to avoid that. It felt out of place to me, especially when it led from the bedroom into the kitchen. I wanted our flow to be similar to the way houses are laid out: entrance > living room > kitchen > bath > bedroom. That felt the most natural to me and allowed us to have a separate private space in the back that we could close off from guests, much like the master bedroom in a house, tucked away upstairs down a hallway.

When we got our Airstream, finished the floors, and started dividing it up with walls, we laid out the space with tape to get a feel for how the layout worked. Ultimately, we needed to see if we could move about and exist in the space the way we wanted to. It also let us see if the rooms we had planned felt the right size (because at this point we could adjust where our walls were placed).

Surprisingly, in spite of all the planning and research I had done to arrive at the plans we built from, the final result ended up different. Opposite is the plan we built off.

Since we lived in our Airstream through much of the renovation process,

we had the unique opportunity to try the space out as we went. Partway through the build we decided to scrap our original plans to install a booth and table in the front of the Airstream. Instead we put in a daybed, minicredenza/bookshelf, and a portable minitable we could use for some meals and I could use to draw on (which eventually evolved into tray tables we could fold up

Our working plan from the day we framed in our walls. It evolved a bit more after we lived in it a while but this was the jumping off point.

and stash in the closet). In most of our previous apartments we tended to ignore the dining table in favor of eating on the couch and watching television (like deadbeats), so why wouldn't we do the same in the Airstream? We scrapped the permanence of a fixed table, which allowed us to use the table out on the patio and inside the Airstream and opened up our front living space even more.

Another amendment we made to our initial build plans was eliminating the shower. We had wired and plumbed our Airstream for direct electrical and sewer hookups, which meant that no matter where it was we would be connected to the grid. That meant we'd be in an RV park or beside a house, both of which have shower facilities. As Brett is 6'2" with the shoulders of a linebacker, he was already having to duck through doorways, and showering in a space he could barely fit into didn't seem very desirable when there would be a building with full shower facilities twenty steps away. In addition, we wanted to fit everything we owned into the Airstream and get rid of the rest, so we found ourselves needing additional storage space.

STARFISH SLEEPERS.

We left the shower pan we had installed in case future owners wanted a shower, built a platform over it and put in a set of shelves and a place to hang our coats. This was the right decision for us and paid off because it meant there wouldn't be any additional moisture introduced into the Airstream through a shower. The last amendment we made to our Airstream plan was swapping our queen-size bed for a king. Again, this had to do with the way we tend to live in our space. I was sharing the bed with all these starfish sleepers, as I've mentioned.

This meant that I was pushed to one edge, bum hanging off the side, most nights. I wasn't exactly sleeping well.

After doing a few quick measurements, I realized that if I eliminated the walking space on my side of the bed, I could rebuild the bed frame to fit a king-size mattress. This was such a great decision for us in our space and made such a difference to our overall comfort and the long-term livability. The final layout of our Airstream looked like this:

A Quick Reference List of Things I Wish I'd Remembered While Planning

— Think about what you need to live in terms of storage: a place to put coats, shoes, tools, business supplies, etc.
— Remember to draw your plans around window placement and wheel wells. They affect what you can put where.
— Where will you live? What kind of hookups do you need? Tanks? Plumbing? Batteries? Solar?
— What are your priorities in a space? Think about how you operate day to day.
— Keep in mind weight distribution and overall heft. Are you living stationary or traveling in your space? Material and layout choices should be informed by this.

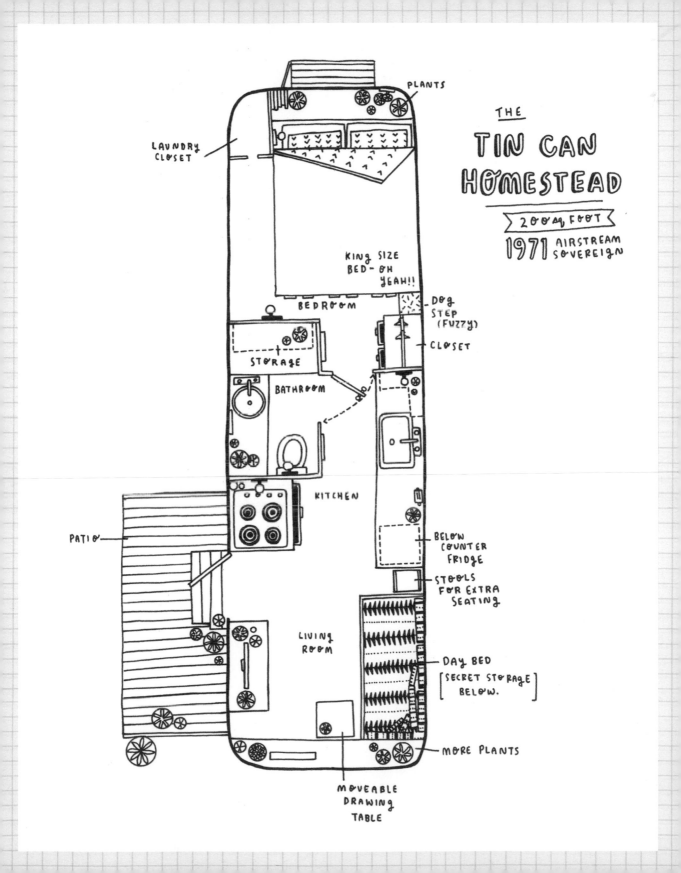

GETTING STARTED

We had our priorities in place. Our wish list in terms of the type and condition of Airstream we wanted and the layout was all firmed up. We ended up finding our Airstream in Portland. We looked at it on a rainy afternoon, and the guy who sold it to us had to break in through a window because the door lock was broken. It wasn't exactly a promising start. When we got inside, we walked around the water-stained plywood subfloor noting the spray paint and mold covering the walls and the leaking windows. It looked as though somebody had been using it as a shed or a place to paint things; it was pretty rough.

We checked the windows, and they were all intact. The floor, although water damaged in a few places, withstood our jumping around on the leaky spots, and the structure had been gutted already with just a few ugly valances still hanging and a broken heater to take out. There was a large hole in the Airstream wall in the back where the shower had been removed.

Although the hole was unsightly, it exposed clean, dry, scent-free insulation with no evidence of vermin or weird odors. We made an offer and bought her. We paid a professional to do some waterproofing of the exterior, fix a few rotting places in the subfloor, and inspect the chassis to make sure it was in good towing condition. He removed the heater, fixed the door lock, and patched a few holes in the exterior.

ABOVE The Tin Can in the shop getting some new weather stripping around the window frames.

LEFT Back outside after getting a waterproof coating.

We also had the brakes done and the external driving lights fixed. These additional fixes ended up costing us as much as the Airstream itself, but for us it felt worth it to be able to begin our renovation with a completed interior shell without messing around too much.

Walking into the Airstream for our first day of work. It looked pretty dismal in there.

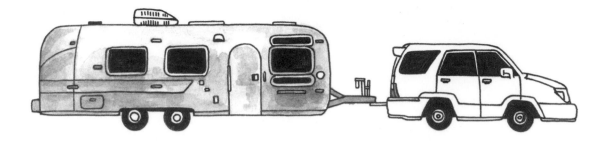

After all the work was completed, we towed her home, which went smoothly until our car died in rush hour in the turn lane of a busy intersection. We had to have a friend come rescue the Airstream and tow her back to Seattle with Brett. I hitched a ride with the tow-truck driver and our vehicle and cried about the fact that he wouldn't let me bring the dogs in the cab of the truck (forcing them to ride alone in our vehicle on the back of the tow truck). It was a bumpy start but finally our Airstream was in Seattle, parked in the middle of the night in the driveway of a friend. We could begin.

The first workday in our Airstream was spent pulling valances off walls, stripping the windows of torn screens, tearing down the remaining blinds, unscrewing superfluous hardware, and throwing everything we didn't need away (including all the bee's nests in the air vents).

We wore face masks to protect ourselves from mold spores and then proceeded to scrub down the entire thing from tongue to tail with a mold-killing solution. When Brett talks about that day, he remembers thinking that we had gotten ourselves into an impossible job. We were broke and scrubbing a dirty,

paint-covered, moldy, aluminum tube that we'd invested most of our savings into, and it was looking pretty grim. I had already transformed the entire Airstream in my mind over the previous four months, so for me, it was just the first step in the process. Still it was cold, wet, and awful work, and wearing those stupid scratchy face masks was no fun. January in Seattle isn't an ideal time to be outdoors in a tin shell with your hands immersed in cold chemical-laced water; it was such a hard first day.

Brett chiseling out the welds on the frame of the old metal hood fan.

Our second day we patched up holes, chipped out weird metal parts that were sticking out of the walls, and ground down protruding rivets. We patched holes we didn't need with a fiberglass patch kit. (I've seen other people get metal squares custom cut and then screwed those over larger holes, which in retrospect seems easier.) Then we sanded the entire interior so we could prime. We also went out and bought a plug-in heater, which we powered with an extension cord coming through the window. I'd done a fair amount of research on Airstream renovation at this point and knew I needed mold-blocking primer

ABOVE Scrubbing down the walls with mold remover so we could paint. It was freezing cold and super messy work. We both had damp sweaters and we left wondering what we'd gotten ourselves into.

LEFT Prying out the old hood fan harness.

ABOVE Ready to prime.

LEFT Patching holes with fiberglass.

that was as sticky as possible to make sure it would adhere properly to the vinyl-covered aluminum walls. I'd read a few horror stories about people who painted their Airstream in the cold and all the paint had peeled off because they didn't prime or didn't let the paint cure in warm enough conditions. I wasn't taking any chances.

We spent the next few days applying two coats of Kilz primer with stain and mold blocker to make sure there was no chance of any old paint blossoming through or any remaining mold spores taking over again. Then we threw on two more coats of latex paint (Behr in Frost).

The paint was such a transformative part of the renovation process and helped us believe that there would be a time when we could live inside this big tin can. It was at this point that I should have built wood covers around the wheel wells, but

I didn't and have regretted it ever since. It made all my other building around them so much more complicated, but we went straight to flooring instead. The flooring was one of my favorite parts of the Airstream. During our van trip I'd spotted flooring in a few boutique coffee shops that seemed to be cut from the end of a tree log, exposing the rings of the tree instead of the wood grain of the side of the log. I'd never seen anything like it and became obsessed with finding it for our floor when I was planning the Airstream interior. We ended up with Kaswell Flooring Systems engineered wood grain flooring bought online, and we loved it. They worked with us from Mas-

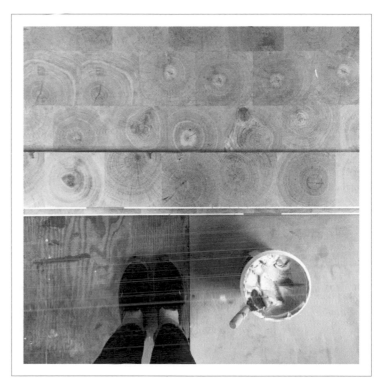

sachusetts to guide me in the installation because I was a newbie. Usually they install the flooring themselves in commercial settings, but I was so in love with the look of it I was determined to do it myself. We wanted something that would be durable enough to withstand the broad temperature shifts inside the Airstream as well as any future building—not to mention our dogs scrabbling around on it.

LEFT DIY install of our engineered end grain flooring. It was our first time installing a floor and I was pleasantly surprised with how seamless it was and how great it looked!

BELOW Halfway through installation.

It was at this point we had to make sure any additional leaks were patched up as we now had three thousand dollars' worth of flooring down that we didn't want ruined. A caulking gun loaded with silicone became a regular fixture in our lives.

All finished!

THE BUILD

A List of Tools Used in Our Airstream Build

GENERAL TOOLS

- tape measure
- hammer
- flat head screwdriver
- Phillips screwdriver
- Robertson screwdriver
- channel locks
- needle-nose pliers
- side-cutting pliers
- cutting pliers
- crescent wrench
- set of Allen keys
- hacksaw
- caulking gun
- level
- wire-cutting pliers
- T square
- carpenter's square
- chalk line
- set of drill bits

POWER TOOLS

- cordless drill (I like DeWalt, but it's a personal preference. Just don't buy a cheap one.)
- nail gun and compressor
- power sander
- circular saw (also called a Skil saw)
- miter saw (sometimes called a chop saw)
- jigsaw
- Dremel tool (for grinding down rivets and cutting off metal things you don't need)
- reciprocating saw (sawsall)

SPECIALIZED TOOLS

- pex pipe crimping tool (for SharkBite pex pipe)
- tin snips
- scribing tool
- tile saw (rented from Home Depot)

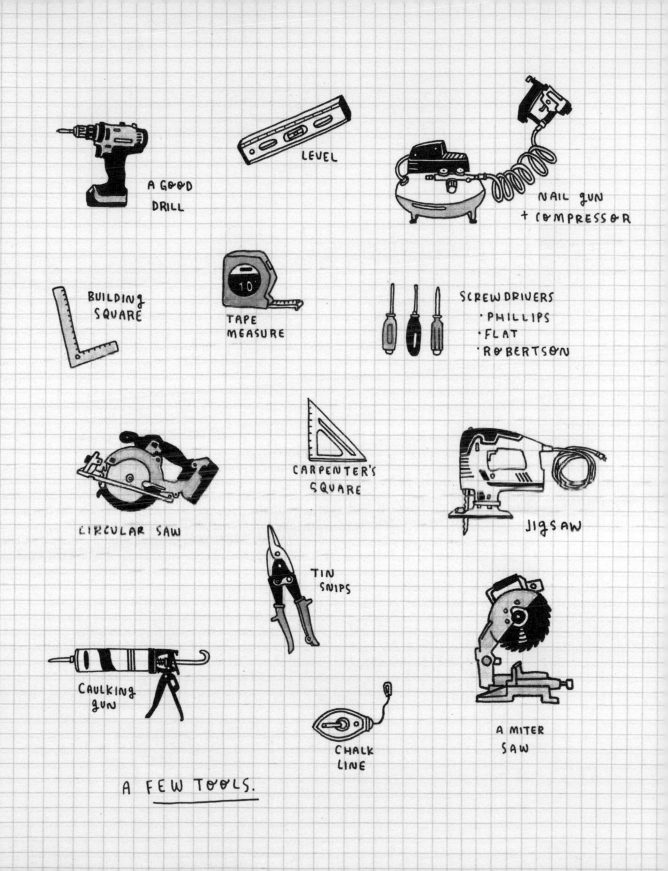

A GOOD DRILL

LEVEL

NAIL GUN + COMPRESSOR

BUILDING SQUARE

TAPE MEASURE

SCREWDRIVERS
• PHILLIPS
• FLAT
• ROBERTSON

CIRCULAR SAW

CARPENTER'S SQUARE

JIGSAW

TIN SNIPS

CAULKING GUN

CHALK LINE

A MITER SAW

A FEW TOOLS.

A Large List of Order of Operations for Our Build

1. Demolition and removal of everything superfluous.
2. Scrub down the walls.
3. Patch walls and sand.
4. Prime the walls with a super sticky primer.
5. Paint.
6. Build boxes around wheel wells. (We didn't do this, but, Lord, do I wish we had. *Learn from my mistakes!*)
7. Install floor.
8. Frame walls.
9. Wiring (install heaters too).
10. Plumbing.
11. Cover interior walls and paint.
12. Install doors and trim for door frames.
13. Add plug and switch covers.
14. Build in furniture.
15. Install sink and toilet.
16. Install appliances.
17. Decorate.
18. Buff exterior.
19. Build porch and stairs.

The interior build of the Airstream was such a long process. I never knew how much work it could be trying to put up straight walls in a curved space. Luckily, my dad is an excellent builder and craftsman and came up once we were ready to start framing. I had decided to use steel studs for the framing, not only because they are light and strong, but also because they're fairly quick to install. They're bendable to accommodate the curved Airstream walls and roof, and wiring and plumbing fits through the preexisting holes. I spent a year as a commercial electrician a few years back and had a lot of experience with them. Since

I'd planned to leave the exterior walls intact and not remove
their coverings, we wanted to do all our wiring and plumbing
through the walls we were building and beneath the Airstream.
So we laid out the floor plan with a square and some masking
tape and got to work.

FRAMING

We used steel studs to frame out the bathroom, kitchen walls, and bedroom walls. I know others have used wood. It's a personal preference, but I like the steel studs. They already have holes to run wire and pipe and are easy to add more holes to using a unibit (make sure you add a grommet to protect the wire). We used self-tapping screws to screw the studs to the walls of the Airstream, being careful not to over-tighten and strip the screws. The other advantage of steel studs is that you can use tin snips to cut out notches in them to perfectly fit the curves of the Airstream.

SNIPPING A STUD FOR CURVES.

Being able to curve the metal was especially important for the roof, as you need to create a curved channel at the top of each wall to fit and screw the vertical wall studs into. We reinforced the walls by cutting pieces of 2x4 to fit between each stud at the top, center, and bottom of each wall, which adds strength and gives you a place to screw into when covering the walls. We used self-tapping machine screws specifically made for use with metal during our framing. They worked wonderfully as long as we made sure not to overscrew them and strip the screws.

Once you're done framing the walls, make sure you walk around the rooms and through the doors a ton. Measure out the spaces for the furniture you're planning on building, and stand in the spot where you're putting a shower to see if you fit. Is there room to sit and stand at the toilet in the bathroom? Lay on the floor where you're planning your bed. Does the placement feel right? This is the time to make changes if things are off because once you run electrical and plumbing, the walls are much harder to move. Did you leave closet space? Do you have a spot for coats and shoes? Always think about the endgame and what your everyday living needs will be.

ELECTRICAL

There are a ton of ways to wire an Airstream, but all of them depend on your living needs. We knew we wanted to live stationary in our Airstream. If we were going to move, we would stay in RV parks, so we wired our Airstream like a tiny home. We didn't do solar or battery power of any kind because we had no plans to live off grid.

Now I need to make a disclaimer here: electrical is a tricky do-it-yourself. It can also be a very dangerous DIY. I had had a year and a half of electrical work under my belt and still had my dad, who is a master electrician, work alongside us and check all our work. He wired our panel and drew our wiring maps. If I was wiring something new without him, I would text him a photo of the tied-in box before turning the breaker back on. If you have never done electrical work before, I would recommend hiring an electrician or consultant to help you plan your circuits and then check your wiring before your power goes live. I've been a part of the Airstream community for some time, and I've seen photos of people's DIY electrical I've ended up messaging them

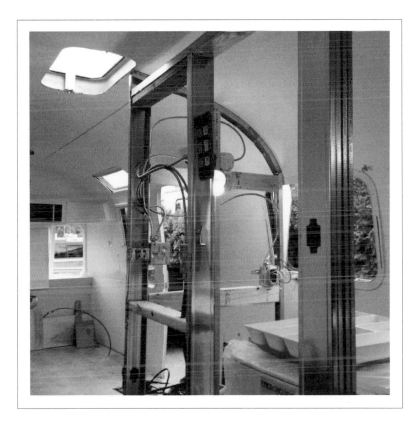

about for unsafe wiring practices. You can watch YouTube videos and learn how to tie in a plug or switch properly, but circuitry and electrical codes aren't something to be careless about. If something goes wrong, it can be dangerous, and it's definitely worth the money hiring a little help. So with that, here's a little crash course on the basics of Airstream wiring . . .

For our Airstream we used an armor-clad or shielded wire. It contains a bare ground wire and an insulated black (hot) and white (neutral) wire. We chose to use armor-clad wire instead of just a regular insulated (plastic-coated) wire for a few reasons:

1. Because you can easily pull it through the holes of the steel framing studs without worrying about nicking the wires.
2. Because it offers extra protection to the wire. Airstreams vibrate a ton when they're moving, and I didn't want to worry about plastic bushings rattling out of the wall and a metal edge rubbing through the insulated wire and shorting out our electrical system inside the wall.
3. With armored cable there are three wires contained within one cable; it makes running it faster.

ARMORED CABLE.

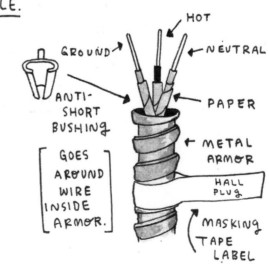

GROUND

HOT

NEUTRAL

ANTI-SHORT BUSHING

[GOES AROUND WIRE INSIDE ARMOR.]

PAPER

METAL ARMOR

HALL PLUG

MASKING TAPE LABEL

Model # HMDR310WE

LEFT Electrical supplies ready to go!

BELOW Tied-in panel and circuit map.

First we decided where to put our panel. We made sure it was in a place where we could easily bring the power in from the exterior. It ended up going in the bedroom wall facing our closet where we could both easily access it and hide it. Then we installed all our light, plug, and switch boxes where we wanted them. (Don't forget a GFI plug in the bathroom!) When you mount your boxes on the walls, all the plugs, switches, and lights should be at the same height—same with same. All light boxes should be centered on the walls and a similar height from the ceiling, all plugs should be the same distance from the floor, and all counter plugs should be the same distance from the counter. Switches should all be at a similar height. Make sure you imagine yourself walking into your living space and turning on a light. Do you like where the switch is placed? Which way will the doors swing? Does it get in the way? These things must all be considered when mounting electrical boxes before you start wiring.

Once the boxes were mounted, we got started running all the circuits with our armored wire. Keep in mind that you need to use different types of wire for higher drawing appliances and devices like the stove, fridge, wall heaters, and water heater. We also ran cable for Wi-Fi as well. It can be helpful to have a roll of tape and a Sharpie around to mark each end of the wire so nothing gets crossed when you're tying in the panel. It will also allow an electrician check your work and help with any trouble-shooting that may need to happen later.

Once the wires are all run, you need to tie them into the electrical boxes. Here's a little how-to diagram of how to tie in a basic plug . . .

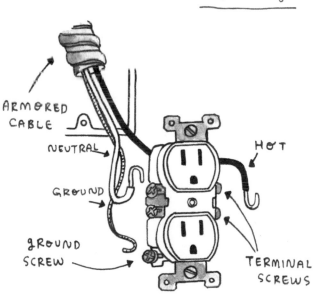

WIRING A PLUG.

ARMORED CABLE

NEUTRAL

HOT

GROUND

GROUND SCREW

TERMINAL SCREWS

A Few General Things to Know about Electrical

— When you strip the insulation off the wire, be sure to use wire strippers, not a utility knife. If you use a knife, you can nick or ring the wire, causing it to weaken and the wire to break off, breaking your connection down the line (especially with all the rattling around that Airstreams do). Practice stripping wire a few times on a scrap piece before you try it on the real thing and inspect the point that your wire cutters hit the wire. If you're making a dent, you need to use a bigger hole on the wire strippers. Once you get the hang of wire stripping, it's a breeze.

— You must ground every box that has a ground wire, and only *one* wire goes under the screw. If you have more than one ground wire, you need to wrap one wire clockwise around the screw and splice them together, which is a fancy way of saying twisting them together (think about the look of Red Vines, perfectly twisted together). Then you need to secure them with a wire connector and make a pigtail (a pigtail is where you add an extra piece of wire to a splice), add a

SPLICED WIRE.

[LIKE A RED VINE!]

wire connector and then use that added wire to connect power from the spliced wires to your plug or switch. It's not safe to put more than one wire under the ground screw.

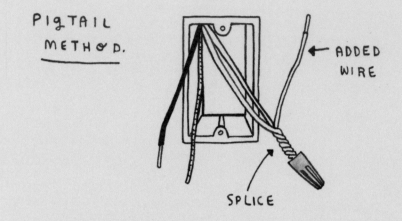

PIGTAIL METHOD.

ADDED WIRE

SPLICE

— When you ground a wire, you need to wrap the wire around the screw clockwise. This may seem arbitrary, but when you wrap a wire clockwise and then tighten the screw over it clockwise, it makes the connection point tighter. If the wire is wrapped the other way, when you're tightening down the screw it's fighting with the direction the wire is wrapped.

— If you're using an armored wire, you need to get metal connectors that hold the wire into the electrical boxes. These connectors come with and without a plastic-insulated interior. If your connectors don't have it, you'll need to use an anti-short on the cable. These are little red pieces of plastic that look a bit like traffic cones with a cut down one side. You insert them between the armored metal exterior and the interior wires to keep any of the metal sheaths from shorting out the bare wires and touching the metal parts of the electrical box.

— When you splice two wires together, you need to make sure those connection points are strong. I usually use a pair of pliers to twist the wire together nicely before snipping off the uneven end and then fastening them together with a wire connector. Your spliced connection should look like a Red Vine, each strand perfectly wound around the others.

— Tuck the wires with their wire connectors back into the box neatly, bending them to fit, before you wire up the switch, plug, or light that will be on the box. This will make it easier to secure the plug or switch into the box with the screws. Be sure the ground wire is tucked back away from the sides of the plug or switch so as to avoid a short.

All these instructions may make wiring sound complicated, and it can be, but you should be able to tie in most of the boxes yourself if you have someone to check your work. Tying in the panel can get a little complicated, so if you're unsure, just get a bit of help from a professional and remember to *label* everything. This will save you so much time.

Because we chose not to remove our interior skins, we ran some heavy-duty PVC-jacketed armored cable (with inner insulation covering the wire) under the Airstream. We chose this cable because it's completely waterproof and protected from road dirt, sand, and water (thanks to my dad for this one). Then, using a long auger bit to drill through the floor of the Airstream and out the bottom, we ran it across the underside of the trailer. This cable going under the trailer allowed us to send power from the panel to parts of the Airstream where we didn't build walls and helped

us avoid removing interior skins. We ran one from the panel to the front endcap, one from the panel to the back headboard, one from the panel to the stove, and then we just ran the rest of the circuits through the walls. This meant that there was a significant amount of us crawling around under the soaking wet Airstream

in the middle of rainy season in Seattle wearing garbage bags. We had one person inside the Airstream feeding wire down the holes we'd drilled, and then the unfortunate person below had to grab it, army crawl to the next hole with it, and then shove it back up through all the layers of the Airstream floor, filling their eyes with dust, metal shavings, and insulation (we usually wore sunglasses for

this endeavor because safety glasses are nerdy and we're obviously incredibly cool, ha ha). Then the person below would use a drill and electrical straps with self-tapping machine screws to secure the entire length of the cable at one-foot intervals to the underside of the Airstream. That way when the trailer is moving, the

Cabinet interior with built-ins with sliding baskets and wheel-well modifications.

wire can't snag on anything and get ripped off. We also ran the Internet cable this way and tie wrapped it to the armored cable.

Remember that in addition to running cable throughout the interior walls you'll need to bring power into the Airstream from the outside. We chose to do that through the floor in one of our cabinets.

We used 60 amp SOW cable or "cabtire," which is essentially a heavily rubber-coated extension cord with an RV plug. We connected the wire to the bottom of the panel and then dropped it to the floor, drilled a hole through the floor inside where the cabinet would be, and then dropped the rest of the wire down to the ground outside. We installed the plug on the exterior wire end and—voilà!—Power! When we need to move, we can just pull the extra wire that runs to the power up through the hole and coil and secure it inside the cabinet.

Remember to check, double-check, and have a professional check everything before turning on the power. The last thing you need in your Airstream is a blown circuit or, even worse, an electrical fire.

PLUMBING

Before we renovated the Airstream, I had never done any plumbing. My plan was to hire a bit of help because it was so new to me, but when my dad was visiting, he told me he could oversee the plumbing and I found out how incredibly easy it was! When I worked in construction, we had a saying that all you needed to know to be a plumber was that shit runs downhill and payday is Friday. I found this hilarious—albeit a little mean—at the time, but after doing all the plumbing ourselves, I understood what they meant. Electrical can go so, so wrong and be very dangerous when

it does, but plumbing is fairly easy to troubleshoot; if there's water somewhere it shouldn't be, you have a problem.

The basics of plumbing are pretty straightforward: water needs to go in and the waste needs to go out. For bringing water in we decided to use SharkBite pex pipe (because why would we ever weld in such a tiny space if we didn't have to?). Pex pipe is basically the Tinkertoy version of copper plumbing. You have a polyethylene tube that you can install in red for hot and blue for cold, and you fit it together using straight or angled connectors. You can cut it with a hacksaw or miter saw and fit everything together before using a crimping tool to make it permanent. You basically can't mess it up (and if you do, it's very easy to fix). On the ends where it needs to connect to the faucets and toilet tank, you push on shutoff valves that turn the water supply on and off and then connect those to the supply tubes to the faucet. Here's a little diagram to show what I mean:

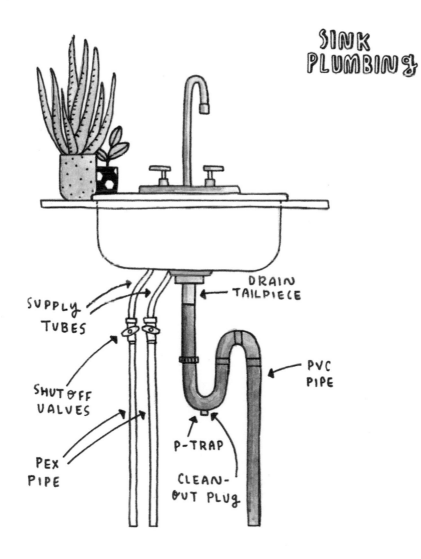

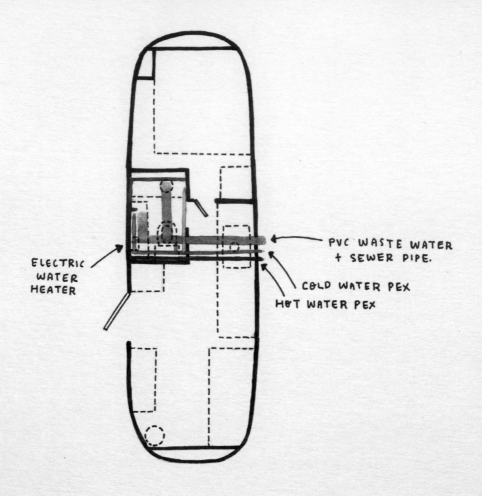

ELECTRIC
WATER
HEATER

PVC WASTE WATER
+ SEWER PIPE.

COLD WATER PEX

HOT WATER PEX

Rough plumbing
layout sketch.

You need a place outside to bring water in—usually a regular garden faucet with a hose connected for potable water. In our Airstream, the hose threads right on to a little faucet under the Airstream. This faucet connects to pipes that are strapped to the underside of the Airstream from one side to the other (more crawling around under the Airstream for us during the install). The pipes go up through the floor into the interior of the Airstream, with the hot water going to the heater, then to the kitchen and bathroom sinks, while the cold water heads straight to the kitchen sink and then across and up to bring water to the toilet, water heater, and sink in the bathroom. The pipes come up through the floor—both a hot and a cold—run through the walls to the toilet and sinks, and are then capped with shutoff valves.

Once your plumbing is all dry fit and looking good, you just need to grab your crimping tool and crimps, pull apart the connectors, thread a crimp onto the pipe, put the connector back in, and then crimp right over the connector. This was a major arm workout and tricky to do under the Airstream and in some of our tighter spaces. If you're having trouble, you can sometimes brace one side against the ground or a wall and use both hands to pull one handle toward the other. Once  the connector is crimped, it's super secure and watertight. If you make a mistake, you'll have to grab a hacksaw and cut the connector off, then splice in a new piece of pipe and coupling to redo it with a new connector. Once a crimp is crimped on to a connector, it doesn't come off, so be sure to dry fit everything before making

it permanent. And that's it for the water part of the equation; now you just need a place for the wastewater to go when you're done using it.

For the wastewater you'll need to install drainpipes for your sinks, shower, and toilet. This is all backed up by an air vent, which goes outside to allow drainage and an air escape so the water

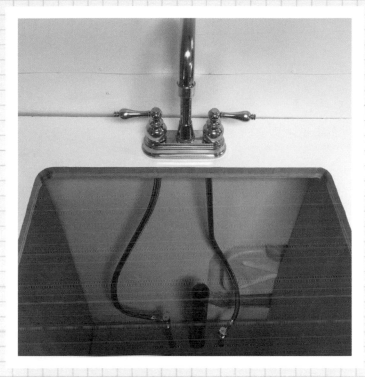

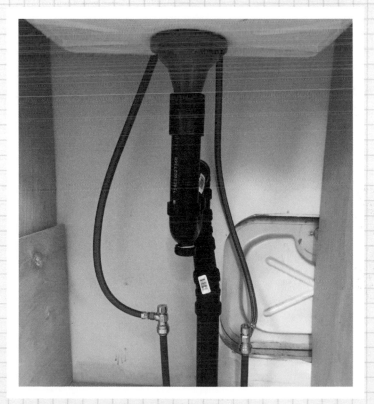

ABOVE Faucet installed for kitchen sink, and supply tubes connected.

LEFT Fully plumbed sink!

flows smoothly and quickly down the drains. We just hooked on to our existing pipe from the old Airstream plumbing system. The toilet flange is installed right on the floor and connects to a pipe that drops to the underside of the Airstream. The shower drain is installed into the shower pan and connects to a pipe that drops below the Airstream. These waste pipes all connect under the Airstream and drain at a slight angle toward the Airstream sewer line. In an RV park you will have a corrugated tube that connects from your RV waste pipe to the RV park sewer line beside your trailer. Since we planned to live with hookups in our Airstream, this worked perfectly for us, but some people who live off grid route their wastewater to holding tanks that can be emptied. Again, you just need to decide how you're going to use your Airstream. In the

preliminary stages you'll just bring water to and from the Airstream because there are no built-ins to install a sink into or toilet to bring the water to. We did our plumbing gradually, so we just installed caps or shutoff valves onto the sections of the pipes that were unused and removed them when we were ready. We had a kitchen sink for about six months before we finally installed the bathroom sink. The stubbed-up pipes in the bathroom remained capped until we were ready to build the bathroom cabinet and install the sink. In the interest of cohesion, I'm going to jump around on the timeline a bit and cover all the plumbing at once.

Installing a Sink, Faucet, and Drain

MATERIALS NEEDED

*Sink, faucet, Teflon tape, hacksaw, pencil, drill and various sized bits,
2 supply tubes, 2 shutoff valves, PVC pipe including P-trap and various connectors
for bends and couplings, PVC cement, miter saw, jigsaw, crescent wrench*

1. Trace the sink onto your counter in pencil, measure the overhang of the sink edge, and cut a hole in the counter with the jigsaw.

2. Drop the sink into the hole to make sure it fits, adjust if needed, and then silicone in place and let dry.

3. Place the faucet in the desired location behind the sink, trace holes in the underside of faucet, drill holes through the counter, insert the faucet and screw nuts onto the underside threads to hold the faucet in place. Connect supply tubes to the underside of the faucet threads (be sure to use Teflon tape), then connect the other side to your shutoff valves (use Teflon tape for this side too).

4. For the drainpipe, you're going use connectors and additional PVC pipe to connect the drain tailpiece (the straight part coming out from the underside of the drain) from the underside of the sink to the floor. Keep in mind that you need to create a P-trap in the pipe and it can't just go straight down to the floor. The purpose of this curved trap is to make a place where there is a bit of standing water to block any harmful sewer gases from rising through your drain. Refer to the illustration on page 77 to see how the drainpipe plumbing should look. Once you've dry fit everything and it looks good, go ahead and use the PVC cement to seal it in place. Putting a piece of cardboard under your workstation can be helpful as the PVC cement is incredibly messy and you don't want to wreck your floor.

LEFT Toilet flange installed for draining.

BELOW Fully installed toilet bowl and tank!

Installing a Toilet

MATERIALS NEEDED

Toilet, toilet seat, wax ring, Teflon tape, hacksaw, pencil, supply tube, shutoff valve,
PVC floor flange, crescent wrench, flat head screwdriver, towels or rags for leaks,
and a helper who is good at lifting things and setting them back down.

Installing the toilet was probably the thing I was the most nervous about doing on my own. But I had a friend coming to visit who was very, very pregnant, and making her walk across the RV park in the middle of the night to pee like we were doing seemed a bit unkind. So after watching a million YouTube tutorial videos, I got down to it.

Generally, when you buy a toilet, it will come in two parts, the bowl and the tank. In addition to that you're going to need a wax gasket, toilet seat (I have no idea why toilet seats don't come with toilets, but they don't), a supply line to bring water from the wall to your toilet, and possibly a flush valve assembly. Ours came with a flush of cheap plastic which immediately broke, so I bought a metal one about a week later and changed it up. Check what yours comes with, they're very easy to change.

1. After installing the floor flange (which is the part that sits on the floor under the toilet connecting the wastewater pipe to the sewer), you need to get the toilet onto it. First you'll put the closet bolts into the flange (this is what the toilet will set into and bolt down with). They need to be right across from each other in a line parallel to the wall your toilet sits against.

2. Take the toilet bowl and turn it upside down (resting it on a piece of cardboard or a towel so you don't scratch your floor) and stick the wax ring around the waste hole on the bottom

(it's called a "waste horn," which I find hilarious). The flat side of the ring should be pressed against the toilet itself.

3. Then turn it right side up (don't set it down again or you'll get wax all over) and set it straight down onto the bolts sticking up from the flange. I needed help with this from Brett because it's heavy and difficult to set down over both bolts in one go. If you place it wrong, you have to scrape up the soft wax from the toilet and floor and start over and you don't want to do that, so get a little help.

4. Once it's placed, fasten the bolts loosely, press down, and rock the toilet back and forth a little bit to get the wax all nice and sealed around the flange and toilet base, and gradually tighten the bolts, switching back and forth from side to side so it is even. The tightening was incredibly nerve-wracking for me; you need to tighten it enough so that it forms a good seal but not so much that it cracks the porcelain toilet base. I ended up not tightening it enough because I was being a wuss, and then when I connected the supply tube and turned the water on, it leaked all over the place. So after cleaning up all the water, I tightened them down a bit more, and we were good. When you've got it tightened up enough you can put the bolt caps on. Now on to the tank!

5. First you add the rubber gasket to the hole on the bottom of the tank, then set the tank on top of the bowl, line up the holes and thread the mounting bolts down through the bottom of the tank into the bowl. Again, tighten the nuts, switching from one side of the tank to the other, but don't overtighten.

6. Install the toilet seat (it's just two screws; you can handle it).

7. Install the supply line from the water shutoff on the wall to the toilet tank.

8. Turn the water on. If it leaks, adjust the bolts. If it doesn't, yay!

You may need to adjust the flushing mechanism and chain length, but that's pretty simple to do, and you've just installed a toilet so everything else is downhill.

Installing a Water Heater

There are a lot of options in terms of water heating, but we chose to go with an electric, tankless water heater. We went this way because they're easy to hide, don't take up a ton of space (because there's no tank), and don't have the leaking issues of traditional water tanks (and because we didn't want to do any propane in our Airstream).

Installation of water heaters can vary, so it's best that you follow your installation instruction manual. You need to make sure when you're planning for it that you bring your cold-water pex pipe in and your hot out of it. You also need to have your water heater on its own breaker because it needs at least 240 volt power.

Shower

I'm sure you've noticed the glaring lack of a section on the shower so far, and that is because we chose not to put a shower in our Airstream. When we initially drew our Airstream plan, we built one in and even went so far as to plumb in and install a shower pan and bring water into the wall. As we were living in our Airstream, though, we found that what we really needed was additional storage. Our shower pan was used to house extra supplies, and showering at the RV park where we were living wasn't an issue for us. Plus since Brett is such a tall, broad-shouldered man, it was going to be a very tight fit. We also noticed that many of the full-time RVers that lived in our park used the facility showers instead of the ones in their trailers because they tend to be very cramped. The final reason we decided to opt out of a shower was the condensation. In such a small space and in such a wet climate, we knew that the moisture from the shower would have a pretty heavy impact on our interior paint job, not to mention the mold and leaking problems it could cause. This was absolutely the right choice for us, but you might have different needs and should plan your plumbing accordingly

A Few General Things to Know about Plumbing

When you're ready to plumb in your sink, toilet, and shower, you want to get your connectors and pipe and dry fit everything together from the sink to the pipe coming up through the floor *before* using PVC cement. Once you add the cement, you can't get the pipes apart without sawing them, so be very sure things are placed the way you want them before you start in with the PVC cement. Odds are you'll do something weird and that cement does set oh so fast, so you'll probably get a bit of hacksaw time in. If you keep around a few extra connectors for mess-ups, it's helpful.

— When you thread a faucet, hose, or valve together, you need to wrap the threads in a layer of white Teflon tape first. This is super quick and serves to provide an extra barrier against leaking.

WALLS

So once everything was run through the walls, we needed to cover them. We chose to cover our walls in tongue-and-groove pine boards for a number of reasons. I liked the woodsy Scandinavian vibe it gave the Airstream, and I also liked the idea of being able to remove walls if we ever needed to (which we've done a few times to add wire for things we didn't anticipate needing since we had no guidebook). The boards were easily installed right onto the steel stud walls we framed, and we used our nail gun and compressor to attach them at the top, cen-

ter, and bottom of each board (that's where the steel walls were reinforced with the wood 2x4s). Now the tricky part is that we were building these walls with a curved top to fit the Airstream. It's one of the harder parts of building in an Airstream, and we went through a little trial and error before we found a method

Whitewashing our tongue-and-groove walls with a mixture of paint cut with water. It was super drippy, but worth the end result. We just kept a lot of paper towels on hand.

that worked for us. We tried a flexible ruler, and that was terrible. Then my dad taught me how to scribe curves, and we were off. It can be a bit tricky to learn to do properly, but once you have it down, it's pretty simple.

LEFT Scribing the curved roof of the Airstream.

BELOW Tacking down a completed wall of scribed boards.

Scribing Curves

1. Start with a short scrap of board.

2. Hold the board in place on the wall you want to cover tight to the roof.

3. Hold the scribing tool perfectly straight with the tip touching the roof and the pencil on the board.

4. Run the scribe along the curve of the Airstream wall, keeping the tool perfectly vertical, don't change the angle at all or your line will be off. This should draw a perfect pencil line that mirrors the curve of the Airstream roof.

5. Using a jigsaw, cut along the pencil line you've drawn and then try putting it in place to see how it fits. Sometimes you need to scribe something twice to get a really good fit, and this is why you use a scrap board.

6. Once you've got a good fit, cut the final board you're going to nail to the wall to length, trace the curve on to it, cut the curve, and put it in place. It should be a perfect fit.

7. Repeat, using the same scrap board along the wall. Once your board already has a bit of a curve it will fit tighter to the wall, making it easier to scribe the next curves.

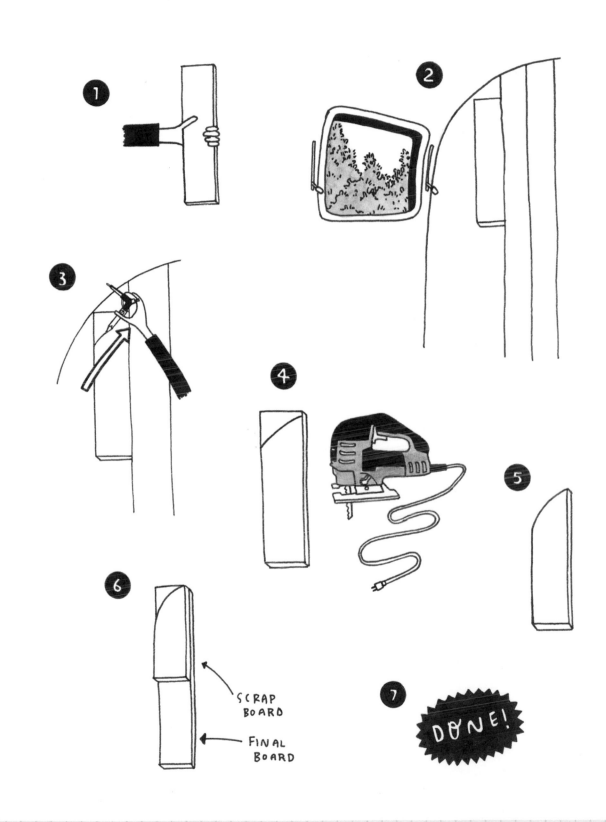

SCRAP
BOARD

FINAL
BOARD

DONE!

FURNITURE & BUILT-INS

By far the most difficult part of creating an Airstream home is building the custom furniture. The walls are all curved, so you can't just put in traditional furniture and have it look nice against the walls without making significant adjustments. We custom built pretty much everything in our Airstream as well as adding two Ikea pieces, which I messed with a bit to make work in the space.

In our Airstream, we built the kitchen cabinets to house our below-counter refrigerator, our countertop range, sink, and kitchen storage. The first cabinet we built was the longest one because we wanted to get as much storage as quickly as possible. I was fairly new to cabinet building when we did this. The only other one I'd built was in our Volkswagen van, and it was a bit of a different look but the process ended up being similar. Luckily my dad was there to guide us. He loves cabinet making and has such a meticulous way of working. The basic building approach

to cabinets is pretty standard, and after that there are a ton of ways to customize them. I've sketched out a basic method with instructions here.

After you've got your basic structure in, you need to do fronts and of course there are a lot of options. In our van we did flush-front swinging doors with hinges, and in our Airstream we decided to do sliding doors.

I chose these primarily because I loved the aesthetic, but for practicality I wouldn't do them again. After living in the space for a year, I still love the way they look, but they're a bit of a pain to work with. You can't get into both sides at once, and if there's something sticking a bit

too far out, the doors get caught up on them. I'm constantly fighting with myself over the balance of form and function in a space
because beauty is so important to me, but in the end, after living
with them for a year, I'd go for traditional cabinet doors over slid-
ers if I had it to do over. I'd also add a few more drawers the second
time around. (If only I'd had this book to consult before I started!)

LEFT Assembling our cabinet walls out of birch plywood and clamping the track down on the countertop while the glue dries.

BELOW Countertop installed, sliding doors in place, all ready for interior basket slides.

Building a Basic Cabinet

MATERIALS NEEDED

¾" birch or maple plywood, miter saw, circular saw, jigsaw, building square, scribing tool, short screws just shorter than thickness of plywood, longer screws for drilling into floor, four-hole L-brackets, self-tapping metal screws, bit for predrilling machine screw holes, wood glue, wood filler, pencil, tape measure, sandpaper. Table saw (optional).

1. Determine the layout of the cabinet and draw your plans. Figure out the measurements and tape out your plan on the floor to make sure it's a good size.
2. Then you start by cutting a long strip (or backboard) that will go along the entire back of your cabinet.
3. Affix the backboard along the back length of the cabinet facing the wall. The top of this piece should hit right where you want the top of the cabinet to be (don't forget to account for the thickness of the countertop you'll add later). This piece will give you something to affix the rest of your pieces to and connects the entire cabinet to the wall. Make sure this piece is screwed into the studs of the wall (in this case the chassis frame) for maximum strength. There should be rivets along each line where the walls are fastened to the chassis which make the studs easy to find. We used self-tapping metal screws to affix the backboard and in some cases had to predrill a hole for the screw because the frame can be a little difficult to drill into.

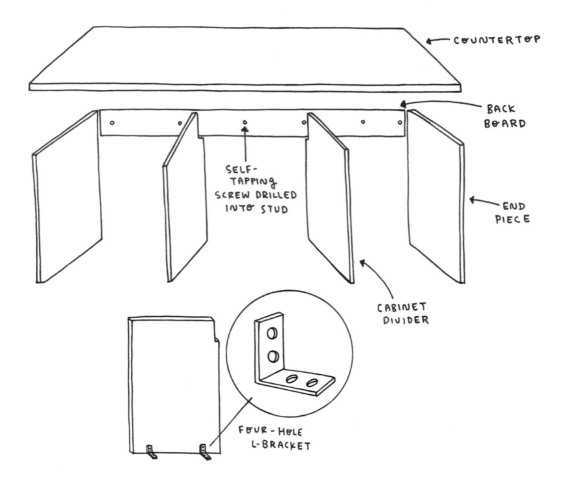

COUNTERTOP

BACK BOARD

SELF-TAPPING SCREW DRILLED INTO STUD

END PIECE

CABINET DIVIDER

FOUR-HOLE L-BRACKET

4. Once the backboard is screwed in, you need to cut the dividers for each section of your cabinet as well as the end pieces. These pieces will have notches at the top to fit snugly into the backboard.

5. You may need to scribe the back of the cabinet dividers to get a nice fit against the wall, but you should be a pro at that by now so it shouldn't be a big deal. Just hold it against the wall, run your scribing tool along the wall with the pencil on the board and then make your modifications with a jigsaw.

6. Using a four-hole L-bracket and short screws that won't go right through your plywood, affix the cabinet dividers into the floor and against the backboard and wall. Use a square to make sure your dividers are perfectly perpendicular to the wall at a ninety-degree angle from front to back.

7. Then screwing into the floor, you should use longer screws since you don't have to worry about thickness (plus it will provide extra stability).

8. Once all your dividers are in, you can cut the countertop. Do a quick measure of your build so far to make sure your dimensions are good. We did a plywood top on ours and lived with that for a while before we installed countertops, but if you've got a wood countertop, you could just plunk it on top and use the L-brackets to affix it. If you're doing the type of countertop that will glue in, you'll want to do the plywood top to give yourself something to glue to. Just make sure you use your square every time.

9. At this point you can customize your interior spaces. Do you need drawers, shelves, a slide out pantry? Think about your storage needs and install accordingly.

10. Now add your cabinet fronts. There are a ton of ways to do this. You can frame out around each opening, then install a door and hinges over it; you can install hardware and then sliding doors; you can do a flush mount front. It's totally up to you.

A Few General Things to Know about Cabinet Building

— When we were doing our build, we didn't have a shop. We would set up saw-horses and our tools outside the Airstream and then tear it all down afterward. This meant that we couldn't have a table saw. We used a circular saw to cut down all our huge sheets of plywood, and although it did the job, a table saw would have been much more efficient.

— Take into account in your planning stage that your countertop needs to have an overhang, the thickness of which will also add to your overall counter height, so be sure to factor that in when you're doing your measurements.

— My dad and I went three rounds over my decision not to have toe kicks on our kitchen cabinets. He was firmly convinced the lack of them would plague me every day. It was an aesthetic choice that he couldn't get behind, but even after a year and a half I'm happy with it. If you want to add toe kicks, just notch out a place for them in front at the bottom and they'll screw right in.

— Plan your cabinet build around items that will go into them. Don't forget to leave space for sink plumbing and appliances and their plugs.

— Some people like to finish plywood edges by using an iron-on wood edging. It comes in a roll with an adhesive already applied, and you simply cut lengths to fit along your edges and iron them on. I like raw plywood edges so I left ours, but it's an aesthetic choice and some might say it looks more finished with the edging.

For your cabinet interiors, you need to think about what sort of storage you're going to need. You'll want a silverware drawer, a place for dishes, food, appliances, etc. How many shelves or drawers? Where are you going to put tall bottles? Garbage? Pots and pans? All these things must be considered when you're thinking about how to subdivide your cabinet interiors. No matter what, you'll probably want to make some drawers. There are a million ways to make drawers, but I like things basic and strong. I'm not a finish carpenter so my method may not be perfect or especially fancy, but it worked for us.

Installing Drawers

MATERIALS NEEDED

Wood, wood glue, tape measure, pencil, miter saw, circular saw, screws, nail gun and nails, wood filler, sandpaper, building square, drill with countersink bit, drawer slides (optional).

1. Decide whether your drawer is going to have slide hardware or will just fit into the space. This will determine whether you need to leave room on the sides for slides.
2. Sketch out your drawer.
3. Cut your pieces to size.
4. Predrill the holes with a countersink bit, using a building square to make sure your angles are perfectly ninety degrees.
5. Glue the joints.
6. Assemble the frame and screw it together.
7. Add a bottom.
8. Insert the drawer into the opening, installing drawer slides first if you're adding them.
9. Center the drawer front on the cabinet exterior and affix the drawer front using a nail gun.
10. Fill all the holes.
11. Sand the heck out of it.
12. Stain or paint it if you like.

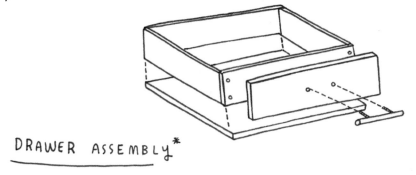

DRAWER ASSEMBLY*

*A HELLA BASIC VERSION

A Few General Things to Know about Drawer Building

- Predrill your holes. When you're working with things on a small scale, you want to always make sure you predrill your holes. It ensures that your wood won't splinter and crack when you drill in a screw.
- Using a countersink bit for predrilling will allow you to completely hide your screwhead within the wood. That way you can putty it later with wood filler, and it will look super fancy.

I like to keep a piece of sandpaper or a sanding block beside the
saw when I'm working so I can quickly sand my newly cut edges
before assembly, this cuts down on a ton of slivers. You'll still get
slivers though. Have tweezers on hand. In addition to cabinets we
also built our daybed, closet bureau, bathroom cabinet, bathroom
shelving, and laundry closet. All our cabinets were made from
½–¾" plywood and were based off this cabinet-building method.

ABOVE End cap built-in to serve as side table for couch and plant stand

LEFT Wardrobe built in. Baskets fit inside cubbies and closet rod installed above.

ABOVE Framing out the daybed to fit the Anthropolgie mattress we purchased.

RIGHT Completed daybed with storage below and lifting lid.

TILING

Despite the perceived problems that can arise from adding ceramic tile to a traveling, possibly vibrating, Airstream, I was determined to have it in ours. I've seen it done in Airstreams and adding a backsplash takes a kitchen to a whole different design level. Of course, there are plastic stick-on tiles available, and while they're a great alternative, the options lack the modern feel I wanted and can look a little cheap. I did a lot of research before I started on my tiling project because there can be issues with grout cracking and even the tiles themselves breaking in half on the road. Although we planned to live stationary, I still wanted to make sure that our tile job was travel-safe. The most important thing I gleaned from all my research was that the tile needs to be allowed to flex and move as much as possible. That meant finding a flexible adhesive instead of brittle grout as well as a flexible grout for filling in between the tiles. I chose a small white hexagon tile, a flexible silicone grout (it comes in tubes in the tile section), and contact cement for affixing the tiles to the wall.

In order for tile to go on permanently, you have to paint a layer of contact cement on its back and then on the place you want it on the wall. Let both dry a bit until tacky and then stick the tile on the wall. Unfortunately, our installation wasn't quite that easy. After I mapped out the backsplash and penciled out the area to be

Before & after tiling the kitchen backsplash. I couldn't believe what a difference it made in the overall kitchen feel. It was definitely one of the pricier aspects of the renovation but it felt really worth it once it was installed.

tiled, I started applying the contact cement to our primed, twice-painted wall. And then, the paint and primer began peeling off the wall. Whoops. There were bumpy chunks of paint all over the wall and bits of the exposed vinyl coating showing through. So before I could tile, I had to paint the entire backsplash area with the contact cement and scrape off the peeling paint. It was definitely a pain, but once most of the paint was scraped off, we were good to go. We rented a tile saw from Home Depot that hooks up to a bucket full of water to allow for smooth cutting. (I would definitely recommend it, and most hardware stores should offer a similar rental option.) We tried one of the score-and-snap tile cutters at first, and it was terrible. We ended up going back to Home Depot, returning the original tile cutter, and renting the tile saw. Once we had the paint scraped off and the right tools for the job, the backsplash was done in a weekend. It was one of my favorite transformational projects, as it had such an impact on the overall look of our space.

A Few General Things to Know about Airstream Tiling

- If you're going with a ceramic tile, choose a smaller tile over a larger one to prevent large surface cracks when traveling.
- Use a grout with silicone for a bit of flexibility.
- Affix your tiles with a flexible adhesive. (We used contact cement.)
- Hand-cutting tiles is a pain and takes forever; rent a tile saw.

APPLIANCES

The nice thing about the way we chose to wire our Airstream is that we could use traditional appliances. RV appliances are specialized and that usually means they're more expensive. For our refrigerator, I knew I wanted an under the counter type because I wanted to keep the sight lines as low as possible so the Airstream would feel open and airy. We decided against installing a stove, but talked about eventually getting a countertop convection oven that could be stowed away for travel and extra counter space. Our appliances were fairly basic, but we happily made do for a year and a half with a half-height fridge, four-burner range, a Nespresso machine, and a toaster.

EXTERIOR

Brett handled a lot of the exterior work on the Airstream, so I'll let him take it from here. — Natasha

After the interior of the Airstream was livable and pretty much squared away, we started on the exterior. Because of the unique design of Airstreams (sheets of aluminum riveted together), they tend to have leaking issues. This is something we dealt with throughout the building process, and we had gotten pretty good at finding and patching leaks. We used outdoor silicone and a caulking gun on any cracks, smoothing out the applied line with a finger. It's a messy job, but now we're leak-free. We always keep a tube of marine adhesive around as well for a quick interior fix in a rainstorm. In the long run it's important to try to get the outside leak spot and not just the interior because you don't want to trap water within the walls.

We also decided to add a custom patio and stairs outside the door. The fold-out stairs that come on an Airstream will do the job, but they're pretty rickety. We wanted to create a safer longer-term solution for us and the dogs. I didn't really want to get into stairway design so I just built a long platform with two stacked rectangles in ascending size on top of it.

The stair boxes were each made separately so that way we could move them if we ever needed to set up in a different configuration with the stairs in a different spot on the patio.

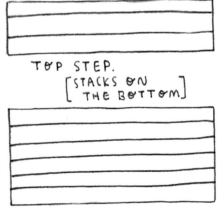

TOP STEP.
[STACKS ON THE BOTTOM]

BOTTOM STEP.

Brett doing some touch up caulking around a leaky window frame.

I vividly remember the previous owner of our Airstream cautioning us on the rigors involved in polishing an old Airstream trailer that had been left to accumulate over thirty years' worth of heavy oxidation. I have never been the type to obsess over the shininess of a car, and so the buffing or polishing of anything wasn't really something I was familiar with. One of the great things about the aluminum shell of an Airstream trailer is the fact that it doesn't rust, and so it is completely possible to restore and polish it to a mirrorlike shine. However, achieving such a shine requires some research and an understanding that the job will require patience and many hours of strenuous labor.

The previous owner told us that we would first need to completely remove the "plasticoat" coating from the aluminum before we could even begin the labor-intensive process of polishing our Airstream trailer. Plasticoat is a protective coating that Airstream started using in the 1960s to prevent the aluminum exterior from oxidizing quickly. The problem with older Airstreams like ours is that the plasticoat

eventually breaks down and can appear quite unsightly as it flakes off and allows for heavy oxidation all over the exterior of the trailer. The aluminum exterior of our Airstream was so badly oxidized that it looked as though it hadn't been washed in years. I still remember the manager of our RV park saying to me on our move-in date, "It looks pretty dirty, who said you could stay here?" For a minute, I thought that we weren't going to be allowed to stay in the RV park that became our home for a year and a half. Thankfully, when I told her we were planning on polishing it, she simply shrugged her shoulders and said okay. To remove the plasticoat, I learned that we would need to apply a coating of paint stripper to our entire Airstream exterior and then use a pressure washer to clear away any residual coating. The Airstream renovation community on Instagram was incredibly helpful at this stage of the process. One couple even posted a video that showed them washing away the plasticoat with a pressure washer. I reached out to this couple, and they were kind enough to recommend an environmentally friendly paint stripper. We bought a paint stripper called Back to Nature from Home Depot the next day, borrowed a pressure washer from a friend, and removed the plasticoat the same day. We also learned that it is much easier to roll on the paint stripper with paint rollers rather than trying to use a brush. To remove the plasticoat you will need paint stripper, paint rollers, a pressure washer, and also painter's tape. One thing I forgot to consider when

removing our plasticoat is the fact that paint stripper can damage plastic pieces such as reflectors and light covers. Unfortunately, we melted some of the plastic pieces on our Airstream a bit, and so I would recommend protecting them with painter's tape before you apply the paint stripper or removing them entirely during the process. I remember procrastinating and dreading the process of

removing our plasticoat, but in all honesty, this step wasn't that difficult as the paint stripper does most of the work for you.

Polishing an Airstream trailer is relatively inexpensive if you do the work yourself. Understand that if you hire another person to polish your Airstream you will most likely have to pay $2,500–$6,000 depending on the length and condition of your trailer. With this information in mind, it is certainly worth it to invest a few hundred dollars in the right tools and simply do it yourself. The tools you will require really depend on the amount of shine you're after. There is a lot of information out there on the correct way to polish an Airstream, as well as the right

Buffing the exterior with the variable speed polisher.

tools to buy, and it is easy to get confused about which decisions are best when moving forward in the process. All I can tell you is what worked for us and the list of tools and supplies we needed for the polishing process. The only power tool we purchased and used for the job was a DeWalt 7-inch variable speed polisher. Without this polisher, I don't know what I would have done. You most likely won't find this polisher in your local hardware store, but will instead have to purchase it online like we did. The polisher will run you about $200 and is the biggest expense in the polishing process. I had never used a power tool like this before, and so I was pleasantly surprised with how simple it was to operate. There is an easy-to-use dial on the top that allows you to quickly change speeds. You will absolutely need the flexibility to switch between different operating speeds, especially when you get into the tight nooks and crannies of the Airstream. The next thing you will need is a good supply of wool buffing pads for your polisher and a backing pad. You will likely need at least five wool buffing pads if you have a 31-foot Airstream like ours. You can also lengthen the life of your wool buffing pads during the polishing process by purchasing an inexpensive spur cleaning tool. The spur cleaning tool simply fluffs up the wool buffing pads as they become matted together with oxidation, which allows you to get the most use out of each one. Of course, you will also need to purchase polishing compound. There are a few different polishes available,

Brett getting an arm workout after polishing for eight hours.

Before and after polishing,
what a contrast!

but I will only talk about the one we used. We used Bright Work polish and were more than happy with the results. Bright Work follows a simple three-step process: step 1 red polish, step 2 white polish, and step 3 blue polish. I had planned on using all three polishes, but after seeing the results we received from the step 1 red polish, we both decided that we didn't want it any shinier. Of course, everyone's taste is different and some people might prefer to go all the way as they pursue a more mirrorlike shine, but that wasn't the look we were after. You will also need a ladder, and I would recommend getting at least an eight-foot A-frame. You will need a healthy supply of old rags to use throughout the polishing process. Make sure that you don't wear

anything you care about when polishing your Airstream because you will be covered head to toe with black grime. I chose to wear black shorts and a black tank top, and that seemed to work out well for me.

I have heard so many estimates on how long it takes to completely polish an Airstream. I would just say that it really depends on the look you are after, the length of your trailer, and the amount of oxidation present. I fully expected the polishing process to take me several weeks, but I completed the job over just a few weekends. I should also mention that my brother gave me a hand with the polishing process and that helped to speed up the job while also allowing my arms time to rest throughout the day as we took turns polishing. I would definitely recommend a good

polishing buddy if you can find one. All in all, expect to spend at least sixty hours polishing your Airstream, and of course the amount of time dramatically increases if you decide to pursue perfection.

If there is one piece of simple advice I could offer, it would be to not polish your Airstream when it is sunny outside. Instead, wait for a cloudy day. I made the mistake of polishing our Airstream when it was quite sunny, and as the shine improved so did the amount of sunlight reflecting off the aluminum. Let's just say that my brother and I had some good sunburns at the end of that first day.

Polishing our Airstream was something that immediately and dramatically improved the appearance of our home. You can pay to have someone else do it for you, but you will save an incredible amount of money by doing it yourself, and you'll always remember the fun you had during the process and take pride in the result every time you look at it.

Polishing an Airstream

MATERIALS NEEDED

Variable speed polisher, wool buffing pads, backing pad,
polishing compound, a ladder, healthy supply of old rags,
leather work gloves, and a spur cleaning tool.

1. Take about a tablespoon of buffing compound and apply it directly to the area of Airstream to be worked on. I wore leather gloves and just smeared a bit around on each section with my fingers. Less is more and a little goes a long way.

2. Using your polisher on a low rpm, work the polisher back and forth across the area to be polished to spread the compound. You want to hold it at a forty-five-degree angle, not flat against the Airstream. Start at a lower rpm and work up to a bit higher.

3. Work in a circular motion on one section at a time, adding polish when needed.

4. Wear sunglasses to protect your eyes from glare and debris and wear sunscreen to protect yourself from any sun reflecting off the surface of the Airstream.

5. When your buffing pad gets mucked up, use the spur tool to clean it by spinning the pad and using the spur to break up the clumps.

6. Keep at it! In about sixty hours you'll be done!

THE COST

Brett and I didn't really have much of a budget in mind when we began our Airstream renovations. This wasn't because we had a lot of cash (actually at that point we were pretty broke) but because we had no idea how much it would cost. I had looked around to get an idea of what people were charging for the shell of an Airstream, so I had an idea for that, but we had no clue about what the interior would cost. We bought our Airstream entirely gutted and then paid a professional Airstream renovator to replace a few soggy sections of subfloor, patch a few holes in the exterior, do a brake job, and do a bit of preliminary exterior

waterproofing (it was leaking like a sieve). We had sold our van and basically used the money from that sale to get our Airstream shell. We figured we'd get as far as we could with the money we had and then continue with the renovation gradually as we continued to make money at our jobs. We also wanted to live in the Airstream as quickly as we possibly could and not waste money on rent that  could otherwise be used for renovation supplies. Each time we got paid, we'd decide what would improve our life most in the Airstream and use our money to do that. We spent a year living this way, and it worked for us.

In retrospect, there's really no good way to work out the labor costs involved in doing such a crazy project right to the

penny. Part of me wishes that we'd kept some sort of log of the hours we put into the Airstream; I can't even imagine how much time we invested in research, material sourcing, planning, plumbing, wiring, and building. Even the most mundane projects like the laundry closet would end up burning an entire day trying to perfectly scribe curves and running out for more supplies or custom fitting one thing or another. Airstream renovations are definitely a labor of love. For the purposes of this book I did my best to put together a rough list of things we purchased for the Airstream to give an idea of the cost involved.

WHAT?	HOW MUCH?
1971 Airstream Sovereign shell	$4,600
Subfloor, brakes, waterproofing	$5,100
Primer and paint	$100
Flooring, glue, varnish	$3,700
Framing supplies	$200
Electrical supplies	$1,010
Electric wall heaters	$100
Lighting and fixtures	$320
Plumbing supplies (pipe, connectors, flanges, pex)	$500
Shower pan	$130
Toilet	$100
Faucets (2)	$215
Sinks	$160
Electric water heater	$190
Plywood (birch and maple), approximately 14 sheets	$700
Tongue-and-groove pine boards for walls	$500
Countertops	$100

WHAT?	HOW MUCH?
Live edge lumber and shelf brackets	$120
Fridge	$150
Four-burner range	$300
Hardware for doors, drawers, cabinets	$190
Doors and trim supplies	$100
Roller blinds	$150
Mattress (Amerisleep King)	$1,600
Backsplash tiles, tile cutter rental, and supplies	$300
Portable air conditioner	$270
Sliding Ikea cabinet baskets	$35
Ikea television console/bookshelf	$100
Daybed mattress	$395
Daybed pillows	$100
Brass Schoolhouse Electric kitchen rail	$150
DeWalt Buffing Polisher and polish	$250
Patio	$100
TOTAL	**$22,035**

It's hard to count all the trips to the hardware store for screws or fittings or a few pieces of trim or lumber. Those things add up, but I'm not much of a receipt saver so this is my best guess. There's also the cost of all the tools required to do such a project. These costs don't exactly figure into the Airstream as a resale asset, but it's a big initial investment and as the renovation progresses through each building stage buying and renting tools add up. Then there's the cost of labor which we really saved on by doing

pretty much everything ourselves. We had a few initial things done to the frame, brakes, and exterior, but after that all the labor was our own. Some people hire out carpentry work, and at $60 an hour those costs accrue quickly. The same goes for electrical and plumbing. I've heard that labor is worth 40 percent of the value of a house, so that's something to keep in mind.

There are some people of course who renovate a lot cheaper, and for some it can be a lot more expensive. Renovations are so unique. In our case we were building our first home. This wasn't a weekend camping trailer for us, so we wanted to create a perfect tiny home for ourselves inside of a vintage Airstream shell. Because of this we used quality materials, and because I love making things beautiful, we furnished accordingly.

DESIGN & DECOR

Designing a tiny space requires a different set of considerations than decorating a large house does. More often than not, the entire space can be viewed from one vantage point, so when you're choosing materials, that is something to keep in mind. You can't really treat a space this small as a set of different rooms with different decor or the place will feel too busy. There aren't a ton of spots to hide things, so owning less becomes important and carefully curating what you do own also needs to be considered. Our position was especially nice in that way because we were able to start fresh and decide what would go into the Airstream piece by piece. That way we could keep tight design elements throughout.

The obvious place to start when planning a space is with the floors and walls. In an Airstream, the walls extend into the ceiling so having colored walls and a neutral ceiling is not an option. Whatever color you choose for the walls ends up being the default color for the bulk of the Airstream. I tend toward neutrals to serve as the backdrop for spaces because it's easy to layer in pop colors later and to change them up when you want. In my research stage I saw an Airstream that someone had painted lime green inside, and let me tell you, it was an assault on the senses. I went with a clean white paint from Behr called Frost and took it from there. I knew I wanted the floors to be a warmer wood tone. On

our six-month van trip I had become obsessed with an amazing wood flooring material at Revelator Coffee Co. in Chattanooga, Tennessee. After some frantic Googling on the part of myself and my best friend, we found Kaswell Flooring Systems which makes end-grain hardwood. They basically crosscut the trees so you can see the rings instead of the usual wood grain. It gives the wood floors a completely different look, and I loved it.

The main living space of any RV tends to be the combination living room/kitchen, so once I decided on white walls and a warm wood floor, I had a jumping-off point to plan the rest. An easy way to find ideas is to do a search on the elements you've decided on and see what designers have paired with it. This is not only a way to find out what you like, but a good way to decide what you don't like. So I went to Pinterest and Google and typed in "kitchen + white walls + wood floor" in search of kitchen inspiration images that fit the bill. I collected those inspiration images and made mental notes about what I was drawn to in each shot. Every so often I would go through the images I had collected

and cull a few that I liked less to help me focus on what I wanted my space to reflect. This allowed me to fine-tune what I would pair with my white walls and wood floors.

At this point I started collecting material samples and combining them into a cohesive palette. You can do this digitally, but often colors on a screen and colors in a space look very different.

Bringing your materials and colors into the space to see how they play off one another is wise. I decided that I wanted wood cabinets and white countertops, and I wanted to keep the fabrics primarily black and white with accents of brass as my metallic.

Once I have my palette worked out and I've made a few decisions, I usually find it helpful to run my thoughts by a few friends whose design eye I trust. In the case of our Airstream

that was Kate from *The Modern Caravan* and my best friend Bethany. Consulting with a creative person with fresh eyes can help generate new ideas and lets you see your plans in a different way.

With the palette chosen, things were simpler when it came down to making the dozens of little choices one has to contend with when ordering and shopping for materials—this is certainly true in a small space like our Airstream, but it can be just as true if you keep to a limited palette in a more traditional home. Here's a prime example of how my palette streamlined decisions: My tile choices were

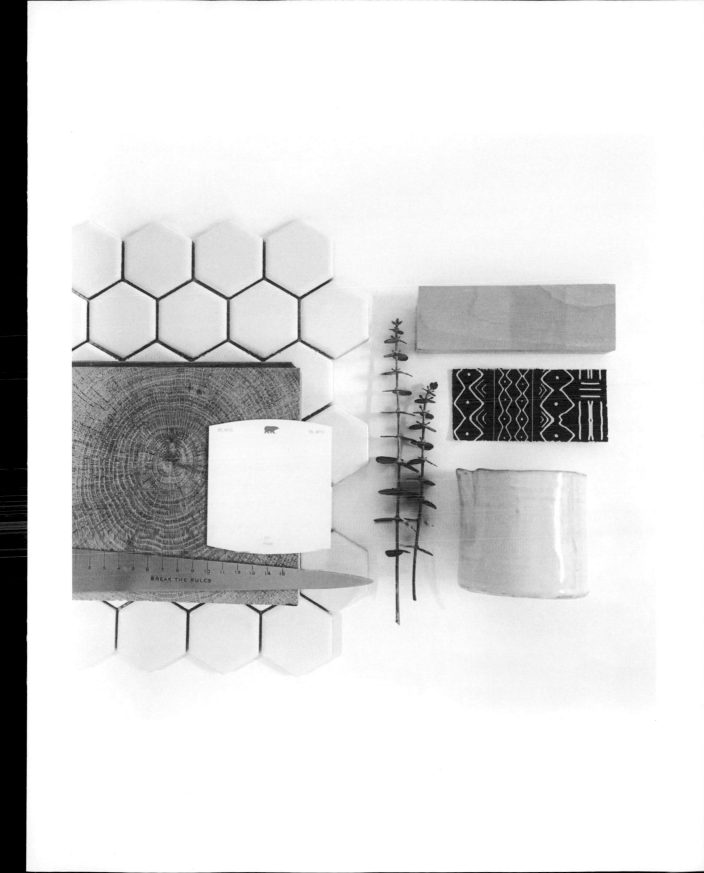

limited to black or white, and my sink had to be white instead of stainless steel because I'd already chosen my metal. Knowing the overall color scheme also made it easy to pick accessories when shopping. All items selected were wood, black, white, or brass, and I mixed it up with different black and white patterns to add interest.

Because I was decorating such a small space, I wanted a tight neutral palette that would carry over cohesively into all the rooms so the entire space would feel unified and calm. I'd begun collecting plants during our van trip and knew I wanted to expand that collection as plants served as a pop of color and introduced an organic texture into our space so it wouldn't feel too stark. When I was

doing my initial image collecting, I found myself drawn to a mix of Scandinavian minimalist spaces and a bohemian layering of found original objects. I love the clean minimalist look as a base for a living space, but I like layering in unique found pieces and plants so it feels warm and homey instead of sterile.

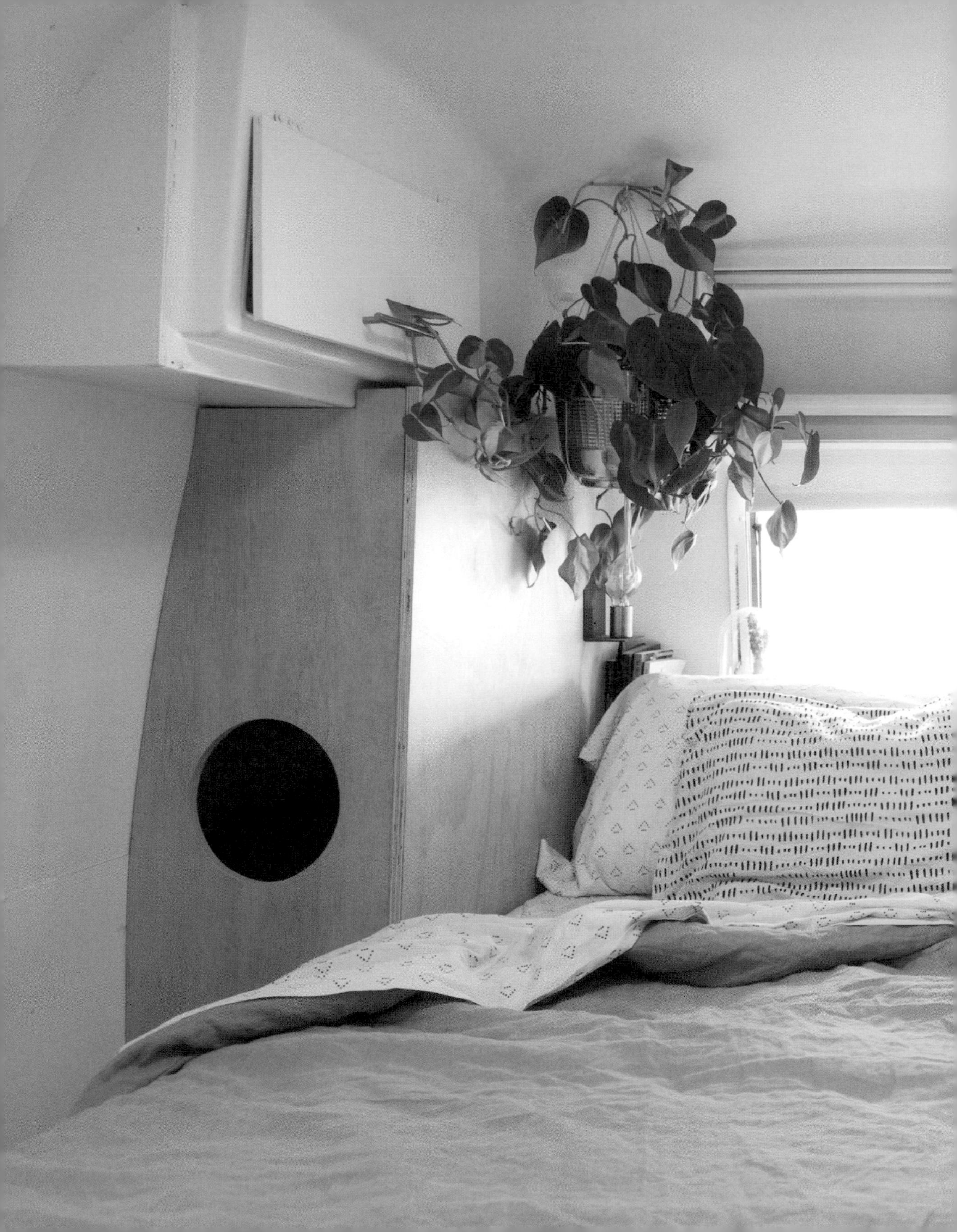

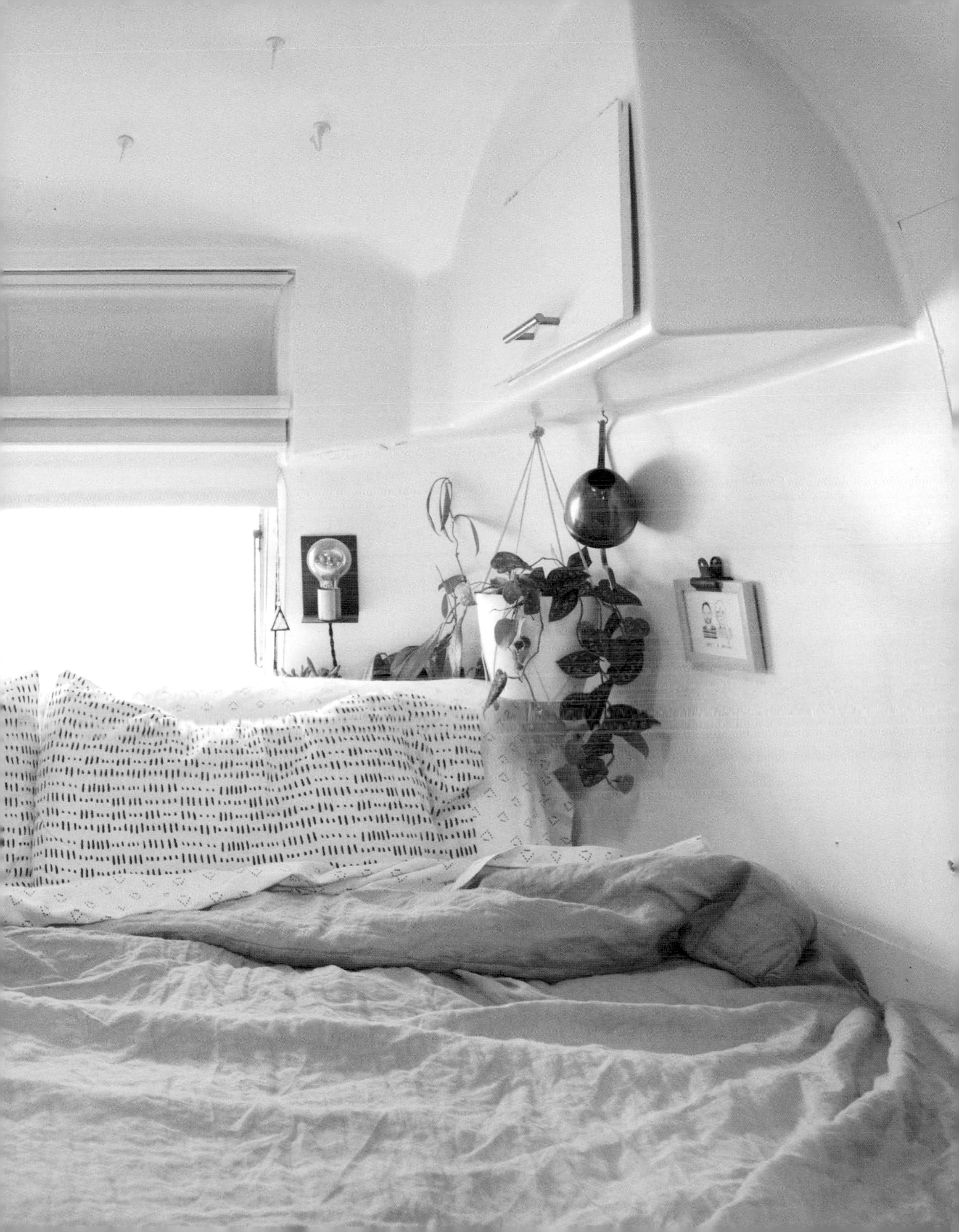

Now comes the fun part—bringing it all together! I built our daybed around a patterned black and white mattress from Anthropologie (a great resource for that boho aesthetic). I selected three different sets of black and white print sheet sets and mixed and matched them. I collected vintage gold/brass frames and vintage photos. I found the perfect white honeycomb tile that was a good price and small enough to vibrate and flex with any Airstream travel. I collected a mix of black, white, and black and white patterned plant pots and grew our plant collection. I sniffed out the perfect gold cabinet hardware that was modern and affordable. I happened upon pillows at Target (a budget friendly option that's always worth checking out) that perfectly matched the fabric on our daybed and added a few black and white mud cloth pillows for contrast.

MIXED FABRIC PILLOWS.

We thrifted some vintage wood bowls and found a few special brass fixtures and kitchen accessories at Schoolhouse Electric—a favorite resource for pieces that add a special polish to spaces. Part of the fun of interior design is the hunt, so wait to find items that make you happy and will add interest to your space. In our case, we gradually layered in new items and artwork until the space felt good to us.

Design tends to be a bit of an evolution, so after living in your space for a while, you may feel the need to tweak it a bit. Sometimes you'll want to add decor seasonally: in winter we put out a knit blanket and pillows on the daybed as well as twinkle lights and a tiny homemade evergreen wreath for the holidays. In

March we swapped the knits out for new dusty sage mud cloth pillows and a linen blanket. Making little seasonal changes like this in a small space keeps it fresh and interesting.

Limiting the amount of stuff everywhere also helps to create a nice space. We're pretty careful about what we leave out on the counters and every visible space in our home is carefully curated. Part of good design is leaving an empty place for your eyes to rest as they travel across a space. If a room is crammed with items in every available nook and cranny, it will look cluttered and disharmonious. Design is about a balance between visual calm and interest.

DIY Design Crash Course

1. Collect inspiration images. These can be from magazines, blogs, Pinterest—whatever works for you.
2. Take note of the specific things you like about them.
3. Consider the walls and flooring, and let those inform your design process.
4. Pull fabrics, material samples, flooring, and paint chips and look at them in your space.
5. Show your ideas to someone whose eye you trust and ask their opinion. Consider the feedback.
6. Start selecting your interior items based off your palette.
7. Have fun arranging your space!
8. Don't get overrun by stuff.

NOW WHAT?
DAY-*to*-DAY LIVING

THE STUFF

When we first moved into our Airstream, our belongings consisted of the contents of a Volkswagen van and our one-bedroom apartment (shoved inside a 9 x 9 foot storage locker). Our end goal was to eventually have everything we owned contained in the Airstream. This meant a lot of sorting through our possessions. On our van trip we realized how little we

missed anything in the storage locker so the idea of going through it felt like a pretty overwhelming task.

We started by pulling as much as we could out of our storage locker and separating the items into sell, donate, and keep. We took photos of things we wanted to sell on Craigslist and listed them, took loads of items to thrift shops for donating, sold CDs and DVDs, and consigned any unwanted clothing and accessories. The entire process took several months and was pretty exhausting, but it felt really nice to get rid of all our excess.

We got to the point where I wanted to burn the entire unit to the ground or just donate entire sealed boxes to charity. I didn't care what was in them; I wanted to be rid of it all! Brett was the voice of reason in this scenario and helped me go through everything.

We wanted everything we owned to be thoughtfully chosen, and I adopted the William Morris quote as my own, "Have

nothing in your house that you do not know to be useful, or believe to be beautiful." In some cases, this meant that we decided to swap some ugly practical items we had for something more carefully chosen and lovely. It was an interesting process but a valuable one in terms of defining our values and spending priorities. For things that in the past I might have just thrifted cheaply and quickly to fill a need, I would instead search for the perfect beautiful functional item. The things around us seem to have more meaning and carry more joy when they're thoughtfully made and purchased. We also tried to use our money to support local artists and ceramicists more often. Living with items that have a story and were crafted by a specific maker adds another dimension to a room, and as an artist myself, I understand how important it is to support other artists when possible.

I'm not a minimalist by nature so this process of downsizing and eliminating was challenging. I've always been a thrift shopper, and although it's economical, it's an easy way to accumulate a lot of stuff quickly because you think less about buying something if it's cheap. The most difficult part of downsizing for me was getting rid of one-of-a-kind items I'd found

CERAMIC COLLECTIONS.

over years of thrift shopping. We got rid of boxes upon boxes of books, but the little strange collected tchotchkes seemed to be what I was most reluctant to part with. I could easily replace books, but unique items were harder.

We developed a few different practices and ways of thinking that helped with all of this. One of them was to channel our collecting into new outlets. We had once collected records, books, buttons, vintage spools of thread, and blue and white mixed china, but all of those things seemed to take up a lot of space without providing much reward. When we moved into the Airstream, we passed on these collections and shifted to smaller and more manageable things. This allowed us to scratch our collecting itch in a small space so we didn't feel deprived or too strict in our downsizing. We now collect espresso spoons, enamel pins, and carefully chosen ceramics.

Tips for Minimizing without Depriving

1. Buy better, not more.
2. Hone your collections for tiny living.
3. Be honest about utility versus attachment.
4. Get rid of unnecessary multiples.
5. Buy items that are not just useful, but attractive *and* useful.

THE CLOSET

Clothing can be a bit of an issue living in a small space, especially for us—we kinda love shopping for clothes. We had to learn to be more intentional and honest about what we needed and wanted, as well as what we possessed versus what we actually used. If we hadn't worn an item in six months, it went to Goodwill. If we had an item we liked but still never managed to wear, we got rid of it. Clothing items that we wore but didn't feel good in also went on the pile. Pants that are too low and always need to be pulled up, shirts that have always had a weird collar or hem and are never quite long enough. Anything that tended to sit in the closet was weeded out as well.

Storing clothes during the off-season is important to tiny living. When spring comes, we pack up our warmer sweaters and flannel, and they go into flat bins under our bed. Summer dresses, shorts, and tank tops go into those bins in the fall. Closet space is valuable, and these little shifts help a lot in freeing up space.

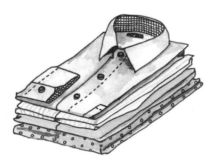

THE KITCHEN

Another thing we've tried to do is buy fewer items, while improving the quality of what we do buy. We try to purchase higher-quality, more aesthetically pleasing items that will last longer (and give us pleasure when we use them). We also got rid of unwanted multiples. We own one good pan and a fancy set of Dansk cookery consisting of one big pot, one small pot, and a butter warmer. We used to have a cupboard full of pots and pans, but since investing in better, more attractive pieces, we use and love *all* of them. When we got rid of the superfluous ones, we didn't find ourselves missing multiples (and we had more room in our cabinets). We also try to get rid of unused items if we are acquiring new ones. One in, one out. We've limited the amount of specific kitchen appliances and gadgets we own. Often kitchen gadgets are used for shortcuts or a very specific task that can be done with a simpler tool. Instead of a garlic press we have a knife; instead of a rolling pin we use a vinegar bottle; instead of a teakettle we use a saucepan. Tweaking the way we use items allows us to get away with less.

We also have to be more careful than we used to about the way we shop for food. We have a minifridge with a separate freezer and a bank of baskets we use for dry goods. Both of those spaces can fill up fairly easily, so we need to plan ahead. We only buy condiments that we use often, and if we can make our own, all the better. Having a smaller fridge allows us to use up items more quickly and prevents food waste as we tend to be pretty aware of what's filling the space.

THE LIVING ROOM

When you live in a home that has less than 200 square feet of usable space, you need to get creative. The only seating in our Airstream is the daybed, which maxes out at three people. In order to give ourselves occasional extra room, we keep a little stack of stools that I thrifted and re-covered with leather, and we pull those out when people come over (they also work great as footstools). We use our patio when we have visitors, for building projects, for creative projects, and sometimes for work or studying. If the objects in your tiny space can be used for multiple purposes, they become so much more valuable.

I work from home as an illustrator part-time, and my drawing
table is also our dinner table, clay studio, and office. Our daybed
can be used as an extra bed and a couch, and it opens up to reveal
a ton of storage space.

THE GARDEN

Since we have the Airstream in an RV park, we had to get creative about outdoor space. We essentially live in a parking space and don't exactly have a lawn or plot of land for a garden. But I was desperate to grow vegetables, so I got a bunch of large pots and a few large metal garden beds and went to work. Our first summer here we planted potatoes, kale, peas, tomatoes, butter lettuce, and

We planted tomatoes, kale, lettuce, peas, potatoes, swiss chard, radishes, and herbs on our little Airstream patio. I had a collection of raised beds and pots from Ikea that worked beautifully and it made us feel like we were homesteading a little more.

a variety of herbs. It was such a great use of our outdoor area and totally freed up a ton of fridge space that would otherwise be used for veggies. When we were making omelets, we could just walk outside to grab herbs, kale, and tomatoes.

It was such a little luxury to have in such a tiny living situation and made our home feel so much homier. When you're thinking about how to utilize any outdoor space you may have, it helps to think about not just entertaining, but also about these sorts of day-to-day uses.

THE PLANTS

A huge part of our Airstream aesthetic was plants. An interviewer asked me how many plants we had at one point, and when I counted, it was something like sixty-three. Then I went out and bought more plants. There are certain plants that are more tailored to specific spaces, and succulents, staghorn ferns, philodendrons, cacti, rubber plants, air plants, and pothos plants did wonderfully in the Airstream. I tend to be a bit of an under-waterer, and these plants generally like to get pretty dry between watering, which helps me out a lot. I often get questions about plant care, so I'm going to share a little list of a few easy plants to take care of and some tips.

Easy Plants

SUCCULENTS. They like at least half a day of sunlight, though more is better. If you see some of your circular echeverias start to stretch out, they don't have enough light. It's normal for the lower leaves of a succulent to die off as the center grows new ones. If the center leaves start to die, then you need to worry. Don't spray succulents with water, wait for them to dry out between watering and soak the roots.

STAGHORN FERNS. They like lots of bright indirect light and are sold in pots when they're young and need to be transplanted and mounted when they get bigger. They like a combination of misting and root soaking and tend to need watering about every two weeks. The more humid your environment is, the less they need watering.

PHILODENDRON. They like a ton of light, but the leaves will get burn spots if there's direct sunlight on them. Let the soil dry out completely between watering, and when the leaves seem a bit limp and aren't standing up straight, it needs water. Overwatering will cause yellow leaves, and under-watering will cause leaves to brown and fall off.

POTHOS. Pothos plants are some of the easiest plants to care for. They can handle low light as well as bright indirect light. I once had one that thrived in a windowless bathroom. They can be grown in soil and easily propagated in water and planted once they have roots. When the leaves start looking limp or brown, they need watering and should be watered more often than succulents and cacti, when just the top layer of soil is dry.

CACTI. The most important thing in cactus care is that they have really good drainage. The roots should never sit in water and they don't need watering very often at all. I water mine once every month or so when they start looking a little shriveled. They can handle quite a bit of sun.

RUBBER TREE. These like bright light (but no sunlight directly on the leaves). Keep the leaves free of dust by wiping them down, and make sure the roots don't sit in water. They need to be kept moist during the summer which is the growing season and then a bit drier in the winter.

TILLANDSIA. They like bright light (but no sunlight directly on the leaves). They can be kept happy by misting with a spray bottle and soaking them in water for a few hours every two weeks or so.

ROUND LEAF HOYA (*HOYA OBOVATA*). They like a lot of bright light but not necessarily sunlight right on the leaves. It's best to let them get very dry between watering. You can tell they need watering when the usually plump leaves start looking a little deflated or withered.

A Few General Things to Know about Plants

– Do your homework and research which plants will work best for your home. A lack of bright indirect light can be a deal breaker for many plants as can direct sunlight on leaves.

– Dust your plants. If the leaves are covered in dust, they can't properly take in light.

– Plants like to be fertilized. I weirdly didn't know this for years, but it seems so obvious now. I bought a squirt bottle of foaming fertilizer (much like the kind foaming hand soaps come in) and followed the instructions on the bottle. You basically just squirt some at the roots and water during growing season.

– When a plant seems to be getting too big for its pot, you can transplant it to a bigger pot to encourage growth. Just make sure you don't go too big too fast or you'll just encourage root growth over aboveground leafy plant growth.

– Be sure to pinch or cut off any dry leaves or vines, so the plant won't send energy to dying leaves.

AFTERWORD

In times to come I think we'll look back on the year and a half we spent on our Airstream with an equal mix of pride and nostalgia. It's the same way we look back at the six months we spent wandering the country in our van. It was such a lovely time in our lives to spend with one another: a time to reset and redefine our priorities and challenge ourselves to do without and to work for what we want no matter how difficult that may be. Renovating the Airstream was such a crazy job to take on, with so much money and time invested in it. But completing it affirmed our mutual desire to take risks and taught us to trust our ability as a couple to handle tough challenges.

When we first envisioned living in our Airstream, it was in the middle of the woods all alone. When we got back to Seattle, we realized that due to the crazy housing and land costs that wasn't going to be possible for us. After living in our Airstream in an RV park just outside Seattle city limits for a year and a half, we found ourselves feeling overwhelmed with the city. We had chosen to live in the Airstream in part as a means of escaping the Seattle tech boom housing prices. Unfortunately, we couldn't escape all the effects of the tech boom. I was commuting to work for four hours some days because of the awful Seattle traffic, and Brett was driving an hour each way. This would be fine if we were in our

We started our Sugarhouse Ceramic Co. business working on a tiny little table in the Airstream but quickly outgrew the space.

dream situation in the middle of the woods, but we were living in an RV park in a dicey area of North Seattle. As Seattle became more crowded, our dream of a solitary life in the woods became increasingly attractive. In addition to that, I took up ceramics the year after our van trip, and the more I made things out of clay, the more I wanted to. Having a studio space of my own became more and more desirable. So we gradually made the decision to look for another place to live.

We started our research, talking about Austin and Nashville and New England. We'd driven all over the United States on our van trip, and there were so many places we'd loved. We finally settled on Vermont because of how much we loved the woods of New England when we puttered through them in our Volkswagen. We researched winterizing the Airstream and began making plans for towing our little home across the country. But as we gathered information, we began to realize that our lovely vintage beauty wasn't exactly cut out for living beneath three feet

of snow for six months of the year. When we'd built her, we'd planned for a mild Pacific Northwest climate. Our windows were single-paned, our plumbing uninsulated. Moving the Airstream to Vermont started to seem like a foolish idea. So, after much thought we put an advertisement up on our Instagram and sold our beloved Airstream two and a half weeks later.

Our shiny little Airstream heading off to new owners in California.

AIRSTREAM FOR SALE!!

Yep, it's true. The Tin Can Homestead is officially for sale. We have some crazy life plans for this year (that we'll share later on) that are sadly non-Airstream compatible, so our beautiful tiny shiny home is now for sale. We have poured our love, time & resources into this Airstream for the last year and a half, and we want to pass it on to new owners that will love it. Our Airstream has been featured on Design Sponge, Poppytalk, in *Sunset Magazine*, and it will soon be featured on Apartment Therapy. We're also in the midst of publishing a book, with a major publisher, about our Airstream renovating journey that will be out in spring 2018.

We designed our vintage Airstream mostly for stationary use, so it would work wonderfully for a tiny house or for light traveling. It would make a great Airbnb.

31 FOOT 1971 AIRSTREAM SOVEREIGN FEATURES:

- unique engineered end-grain wood flooring from Kaswell Flooring Systems
- custom birch ply built-in cabinets, daybed, laundry closet, endcap & headboard
- 6-month-old king-size Amerisleep memory foam bed (happy to take it if you don't want it though)
- brass faucet & ceramic kitchen sink with hexagon tile backsplash
- brass faucet & ceramic bowl sink in bathroom
- porcelain toilet
- portable AC unit
- four-burner range
- live-edge wood kitchen shelving
- Anthropologie daybed mattress & matching pillows
- 120v wiring

- electric wall heaters in front and rear
- residential plumbing with direct hookups (water & waste tanks could be added for off-grid use if desired. Currently there is no shower but the shower pan is plumbed and installed and water is plumbed into the wall as well. We installed temporary shelving instead of a shower but that could be changed to suit your needs.)
- custom skylight and roller shades on all windows
- flash electric water heater
- @schoolhouse brass kitchen rail with hooks & Edison bulb bedroom sconces
- new trailer brakes
- door-mounted Letterfolk message board
- will include 5 potted plants :)

Remember that this is a vintage Airstream with little quirks; it is by no means perfect but we love it! We're located in Seattle, WA. Pick up only. Possession date negotiable (it's our home & we need to move out first!). We'll have it professionally cleaned before handing it over.

Direct message or e-mail for additional inquiries.

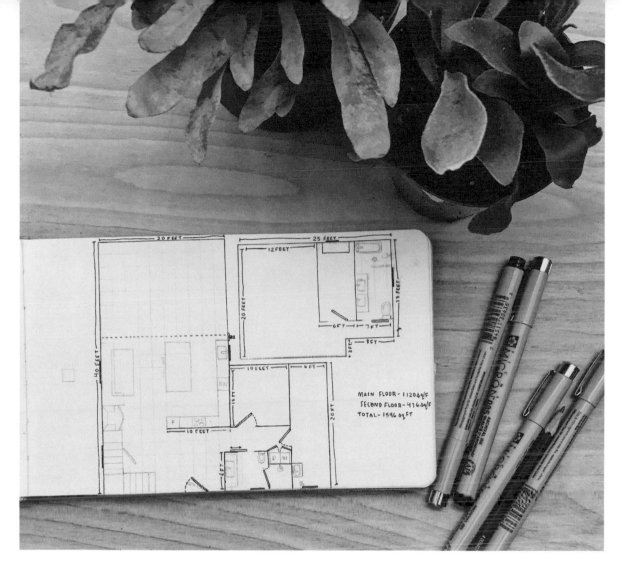

Our plan was to buy a piece of land in Vermont and carve out a little place for ourselves in the woods. With renewed vigor we brushed off our dream of building a cabin and began to plan our sojourn. For the price of twenty acres of land in Vermont you can't even buy a crummy condo in Seattle, so everything felt right to us. We researched, sketched, and drafted plans for a little cottage and ceramics studio in the woods. We flew out to Vermont and looked at properties, and we planned and planned.

At the same time we finish writing our book, we're packing up
our life in the Airstream to get it ready for its new owners. A month
from now the Tin Can Homestead Airstream will be shipped to
California to meet them, and we will head out to Vermont with
all our possessions packed into our pickup, looking for our own
little patch of land. For more about our airstream renovation you
can find us on Instagram at @tincanhomestead and if you want
to catch up with our latest adventures at our Vermont homestead
check us out on Instagram at @sugarhousehomestead.

GLOSSARY

ARMORED CABLE: An electrical conducting cable that is covered with a flexible metal protective cover.

CHASSIS: The base frame of an Airstream comprised of a metal chassis made up of a long oval frame with crossbars. It looks a bit like the skeleton of a whale.

COUNTERSINK BIT: A tool for creating an indent in the wood over a drilled hole so the screwhead is flush or below the surface of the wood.

COUPLING: A connector for joining two pieces of two items.

DRY FIT: To fit pieces together before permanently gluing to make sure they are cut to size and will assemble properly.

FLUSH: When something is made to be fit evenly into whatever it is installed into. I like when you fit a peg into a hole and can perfectly run your finger from one side across the top of it to the other without feeling a bump because it's *flush*.

A FLUSH SCREW.

HACKSAW: A saw for cutting metal, consisting of a long narrow blade in a fixed frame.

JIGSAW: An electric machine saw with a narrow vertical blade for cutting curves or patterns.

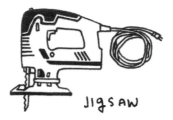

JIGSAW

MITER SAW: More commonly called a chop saw. It's a saw used for quick cutting wood to length. It can also cut angles.

A MITER SAW

PIGTAIL: One wire, spliced into two others and connected to join several currents into one wire.

PIGTAIL METHOD.

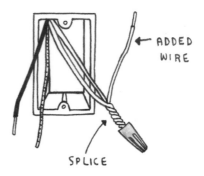

← ADDED WIRE

SPLICE

PLASTICOAT: Plastic coating on the exterior of Airstreams starting in the 1970s.

P-TRAP: A curved bit of pipe installed under a sink that traps a bit of water in the pipe, used to help block methane sewer gases from coming up the pipe.

PVC: A plastic compound called polyvinyl chloride used for construction materials to make plumbing pipes and coated electrical wire.

SCRIBE OR SCRIBING TOOL: A hand tool used to trace the curve from one shape onto another.

SHORTING OUT: An electrical term for creating a short circuit.

SHUTOFF VALVE: A valve used to open and close a pipe to prevent or enable water flow.

SKIL SAW: A portable electric saw, correctly termed a circular saw.

CIRCULAR SAW

SPLICE: To join wire by interweaving the strands.

SQUARE: Oddly named because they're shaped like triangles but a building square is used to make sure two pieces that fit together are at a perfect ninety-degree angle.

BUILDING SQUARE

STUBBED UP: When a pipe is pushed up through the bottom of the floor and sticks up a few inches above the surface with a cap on it. Usually done when plumbing to allow water flow to come to some areas and restrict it from others until plumbing fixtures are installed.

SUBFLOOR: The thick treated plywood floor that's installed over the Airstream chassis. It is the base for installing whatever flooring you choose on top of it.

T SQUARE: A T-shaped building tool used for testing right angles and used to measure ninety-degree lines across large pieces of plywood.

TYING-IN: Electrical slang, referring to the act of terminating wires into electrical boxes or panels to create circuits.

UNIBIT OR STEP-BIT: A specialized bit used to drill $\frac{3}{16}$- to $\frac{7}{8}$-inch holes through steel studs. We used these to run wires and plumbing through our steel studs after framing.

SOURCING LIST

PAINTS & COLORS
Behr Frost

LIVING ROOM
Black mud cloth pillows: Mae Woven

Brass lamp: Target

Daybed mattress: Anthropologie with matching pillows from Target

Green mud cloth pillows: Territory Home Goods

KITCHEN
Artwork: Banquet Workshop (cactus) and Kristen Barnhart (ladies)

Brass rail hanger: Schoolhouse Electric

Faucet: Kingston Brass

Hexagon tile: Home Depot

Sconces: Ikea

Shelf: custom live-edge wood and Ikea brackets

Sink: Ikea

Toaster: Bella

MASTER BEDROOM
Artwork: Anthony Burrill for Schoolhouse Electric

Bed: Amerisleep

Bedding: Nate Berkus for Target

Sconces: Schoolhouse Electric

BATHROOM
Faucet: Kingston brass

Lamp: Target

Sconce: Ikea

ABOUT *the* AUTHORS

Natasha is an illustrator by trade and brought her skills as a former designer at Anthropologie to the Airstream project. She grew up woodworking with her dad and worked as an apprentice electrician for a while. She has always had a love of beauty and design and is the aesthetic force and builder behind the Airstream. She has lately taken up ceramics, and she and Brett have plans to run a ceramics business out of their new Vermont homestead. Brett works with special needs students and has a degree from Western Washington University in social work. He is a dreamer and wanderer and in many ways the impetus for their creative lifestyle. He has worked as Natasha's assistant and support and has been expanding his building skills throughout their Airstream process. He took his first pottery class at the end of his degree and has recently joined Natasha in her ceramics business. They have been together for four years and live in Vermont with their two tiny Yorkies. They spend their free time together drinking coffee, taking pictures, making pottery, and discussing the destination of their next trip.

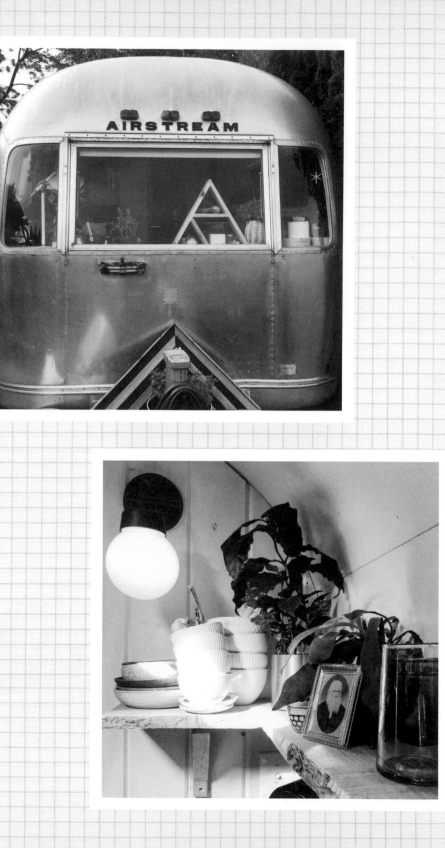

ACKNOWLEDGMENTS

This book couldn't have happened without the help of my Dad, without whom I wouldn't have the skills to build anything. We would also like to thank *The Modern Caravan* for their inspiration, and for giving us the idea in the first place: they do it better and they do it often. And finally, to all the lovely people who have been so interested and invested in our crazy journey. There's definitely more to come.

— Natasha & Brett

INDEX

O

Odors, 17, 35

Off-grid living, 18, 24, 59, 84

Oliver, Kate, 9, 10, 15, 152

Outdoor space
    garden, 180–183
    patio, 30, 54, 123–125, 145, 176,
        181–182, 190
    stairs, 123–125

Oxidization, 124–126

P

Painting tips, 42–45, 54, 119, 127, 130

Parking concerns, 14–15, 23–24

Patio, 30, 54, 123–125, 145, 176,
    181–182, 190

Planning checklists, 17–18, 32

Planning process, 23–33, 149–151

Plants, 155, 159, 184–190

Plasticoat, 124–127, 130

Plumbing, 30–32, 54–55, 75–91

Polishing costs, 130–132

Polishing techniques, 123–138

Porch, 54. *See also* Patio

Prasse, Ellen, 9, 15

Priorities, 14–18, 23–33, 35, 168–169, 191

Propane, 18, 27, 89

R

Range, 99, 121, 145

Refrigerator, 65, 99, 121, 145, 175

Renovations
    build process, 51–147
    built-ins, 99–114
    cabinets, 99–114
    cleaning up after, 23–24
    closets, 64, 112–113
    costs of, 140–147
    flooring, 46–49, 144, 150–151
    framing, 57–58
    furniture, 99–114
    initial renovations, 35–42
    mold removal, 38, 42–45
    order of, 54
    painting, 42–45, 54, 119, 127, 130
    patching holes, 35, 42–44, 54, 141
    patching leaks, 49, 87–88, 123
    planning, 15, 19, 23–24
    plumbing, 30–32, 54–55, 75–91
    storage spaces, 99–114
    tile, 116–120
    walls, 57–58, 93–97
    water damage, 17, 18, 35
    wiring, 30–32, 54–56, 59–74

RV parks
    finding, 14–15, 23
    living in, 23–24, 30–31, 87–91,
        126–127, 180–183, 191–192
    outdoor space in, 180–183
    researching, 14–15, 23–24
    utility hookups, 30–32, 84–85